MUSIC EDUCATION

MUSIC EDUCATION
Tradition and Innovation

By

ROBERT WALKER

**Ph. D., B. Mus.,
A.R.C.M., A.R.C.O.**

*Associate Professor
Faculty of Education
Simon Fraser University
Burnaby, British Columbia, Canada*

CHARLES C THOMAS • PUBLISHER
Springfield • Illinois • U.S.A.

Published and Distributed Throughout the World by

CHARLES C THOMAS • PUBLISHER

2600 South First Street

Springfield, Illinois 62717

© *1984 by* CHARLES C THOMAS • PUBLISHER

ISBN 0-398-04861-4

Library of Congress Catalog Card Number: 83-4672

Printed in the United States of America

Q-R-3

Library of Congress Cataloging in Publication Data

Walker, Robert, 1946-
  Music education.

  Bibliography: p.
  Includes index.
    1. School music — instruction and study. 2. Music
Instruction   and   study   —   Juvenile.   3. Education,
Elementary.
  I. Title.
  MT1.W3   1984   372.8'7   83-4672
  ISBN 0-398-04861-4

To Pam, whose sharp and incisive musical intelligence has been an inspiration for this book.

INTRODUCTION

A book about music education is also a book about music. What is music? Some would say it is Beethoven's Ninth Symphony, Mozart's Symphony no. 40 in G Minor, Monteverdi's "Vespers," or Bartok's "Music for Strings, Percussion and Celeste," not to mention Mahler's *Resurrection* Symphony, Boulez's "Le Marteau," or Tallis's "Spem in Alium," a Javenese gamelan, an Indian potlatch dance, a Bulgarian folk song, etc. The list could go on to include the Manhattan Transfer performing their version of "Birdland," Luciano Pavarotti singing in *La Boheme*, and Leonard Bernstein conducting Mahler's *Resurrection* Symphony. Already something of the complexity of music emerges from all this. We cannot just say music is Mozart's Symphony in G Minor, for we could not be wholly satisfied hearing it performed by a group of people picked at random from the sidewalk of some large city, unless by some miraculous chance they all happened to belong to the New York Philharmonic Orchestra, the London Symphony, or the Berlin Philharmonic Orchestras. Neither can we be satisfied with Pavarotti performing a potlatch dance, or a Javenese gamelan orchestra playing Mozart's Symphony no. 40.

Music means a satisfying and culturally appropriate performance of the work in question, and satisfying means performing at a standard good enough to take our attention away from technical inadequacies to allow us to concentrate on the musical statements being realized in sound. In this way there would be few who could do much to impress us in performances of "Birdland" as do the Manhattan Transfer, and you might easily exchange Placido Domingo for Luciano Pavarotti in _La Boheme_ (and here some partisan listeners would protest) but few others. Culturally appropriate signifies the central importance of different cultural milieux in shaping different types of music. Not only is it bizarre to imagine a Javenese Gamelan orchestra performing music from a bygone age of European artistrocratic priviledge, but some might even scoff at the idea of a non-Italian having the temerity to sing Verdi or Puccini at La Scala Milan. Such are the significance of social and cultural imperatives in musical practices.

It is possible to deduce from this that music involves a combination of a number of things: an original idea, i.e. a composition or improvisation, a performance of it by performers who have technically high standards and somehow have the ability to enter into the spirit of the original idea in such a fashion as to communicate that "something special" to those listening, and finally, listeners with the conceptual ability to appreciate both the original musical idea and the concretization of it into sound by performers who are perceived to have appropriate abilities, both technical and empathetical. Here is a complex web of interaction between composer or originator, performer, and appreciator.

What should music education be concerned with? One thing emerges: It is possible to identify different functions or different types of goals within music education. From the above argument there are at least three, composing, performing, and listening. Presumably a completely educated musician has achieved suitable goals in all three! In what we call Western culture there are institutions offering specialist musical education for those who can demonstrate a suitable level of competence initially to be eligible for entry to such an education (it certainly is not for everyone): the Juillard School in New York, the Royal College in London, or the Paris Conservatoire are examples of such institutions, and their products fill the desks in the world's major orchestras, etc. In some other cultures musical practices are handed down as part of an oral tradition relating to a particular cultural milieu from one generation to another sometimes with little modification. In Western culture and other cultures influenced by the explosion of science, technology, and social change, there is continual modification in the light of new ideas concerning both performance of music and the nature of music itself.

Since this book is concerned with music education in elementary schools, the three goals mentioned above relating to a completely educated musician perhaps provide something of a starting point in identifying appropriate strategies, goals, and content for an education in music in an elementary school. It must also be concerned with the modifications referred to, as the world's cultures evolve from one state of awareness to others. There are certain assumptions underlying the three goals related to aesthetic values and cultural norms, and they need examining in critical fashion. Also, aims of a general education are not irrelevant, for although many feel that somehow music is special, different, and in a class of its own, it has to be placed within a context of an educational philosophy that relates to all areas of the curriculum and to a higher order of general educational goals. To this end various chapters take a deliberately objective standpoint on some matters of both musical and educational concern, for it is felt necessary to examine historical and current practices in music education critically.

The aim of the book is to brush away the cobwebs, to examine what has been done and why, what is done, and what might best be done in the music classroom of the elementary school and, it is hoped, to provide some reference points to help those concerned with music education generally.

It is felt that the best way to achieve this is to approach the task in the manner suggested by Wittgenstein:

> One must begin with the error and lead it to the truth, that is, one must uncover the source of error: otherwise hearing the truth won't help us. It cannot penetrate when something else is taking its place. To convince someone of the truth it is not enough to state it; but one must find the *path* from error to truth. (Norman Malcolm, *Wittgenstein: A Memoir.*, 1967.)

CONTENTS

MUSIC EDUCATION

EDUCATION AND MUSIC

W ITH the growth of mass education and state control has developed a notion that education as a process only takes place within one or more of the institutions that exist to educate. We talk of someone as being educated only if he or she has attended certain institutions and has been given their seal of approval, i.e. various certificates, diplomas, and degrees. The very word *education* has acquired a connotation that is strictly concerned with formalised, institutionalised instruction and learning.

With this development coexists a fundamental weakness. Formalised institutions necessitate organisational structures, program planning, management, and accountability. These are all deemed essential as far as the operation of an institution is concerned, but inevitably they take their toll on educational content. Decisions have to be made because of limits in resources, expertise, or declared aims, and decisions mean approvals and consequent disapprovals. This would be no large problem if the content of education were some finite quantity concerning unchangeable perceptions of objects and facts; approvals could be refined to the point of ensuring the retention of the best and the rejection of the worst according to some established criteria.

However, the content of education is anything but finite and unchangeable, and the biggest problem facing any institution or organisation involved in education concerns its response to this. No subject area of the curriculum can be said to be finite and unchangeable. It follows, therefore, that administrative structures need to be flexible enough to accommodate an ever increasing rate of change in the quantity and quality of knowledge and experience or run the risk of charges of irrelevance from the consumer. In some subject areas the rate of discovery is so rapid that almost any planning of educational content for teaching is almost certain to be overtaken by events before implementation. In other areas opinions and attitudes are important, but they are subject to change as the new challenges the established. Music and the arts generally are in this category. What constitutes good music in Western culture is a question that has only been satisfactorily answered for historical music. Sources indicate that during the last two or three hundred years some artists have not been accorded the same contemporary evaluation of their worth as that by commentators in posterity. This is because of changing criteria and standards of qualitative evaluations of aesthetic experience. Naturally, as such evaluations became more refined and sophisticated so did the chances of being recognized adequately by one's contemporaries increase. The main reason for retrospective judgements being more favourable for some lies in the development of this field.

Educational institutions are apt to rely on historical music because of the relative reliability of qualitative comment on it. Consequently, some tend to ignore contemporary music and its apparently bewildering variety of styles and fashions. Moreover, there is a strong feeling generated that music of the past is preferable to music of the present among people generally as a result of this situation.

By historical tradition music has held an important place in education. From ancient times to the present it has been held in awe as something possessing, variously, the power to unfold ultimate mysteries, therapeutic values, and hypnotic or civilising properties upon the general populace. Even the explosion of scientific enquiry sparked by the Renaissance and its aftermath has not entirely dispelled this belief about music and its powers, such is the extent of the influence of traditional values in music.

Nowadays contemporary music struggles for acceptance though

not for survival; acceptance by the institutions, that is, but survival is ensured by the popularity of its various styles among the differing groups of their adherents.

The effect of this upon education, necessarily conservative and cautious in its content and structures, thereby sometimes lacking the vitality of contemporary live events, is to leave music teachers with little or no choice but to play safe with historical music, the estimated value of which provokes little controversy. The issue of relevance thus becomes of some importance in educational use of an art form such as music, which plays such a prominent role in everyday life as distinct from its uses in education. It is perhaps important to state the obvious, that students will always attempt to reconcile their perceived experience of events contemporary with their existence with reality as perceived in educational institutions. In the case of music this means, more often than not, reconciling their day to day experience of contemporary music with what appears to be a more fossilised offering in the educational institution, where notions of quality and taste sometimes seem spurious to the student and appear to confound the commonsense dictates of daily experience.

The historical slant is plain from many publications currently in use in schools in teaching music. Children sing historical songs, play historical tunes on instruments, and learn historical notations. Children are rarely taught values, however, even if they are retrospective judgements of historical music. Children capable of assimilating the value-laden content of films such as *Star Wars* or *E. T.* could also benefit from learning about artistic politics. For example, W.A. Mozart is now universally accepted as a "great" composer, but during his life he struggled for recognition, dying with little or no true appreciation from many of his contemporaries. Admitted, he died very young, and had he lived longer he would have enjoyed some of the fame his music subsequently earned. Nevertheless, he had written his masterpieces before he died and they were not then appreciated as much as the works of some of his now downgraded contemporaries. Some other composers can be cited as suffering similar deprivation during their lives in startling contrast to the views of posterity. Chief among these must be J.S. Bach, perhaps the most spectacularly misunderstood and almost certainly a victim of the new and conflicting aesthetic theories of the eighteenth century "style galant."

Despite such rationalisations of the plight of victims of artistic politics and the subsequent reappraisal from posterity, the myth lives on about alleged superiority of historical idioms. The issue of quality remains a neglected one, however, in comparison with the emphasis placed upon simple acts of literate behavior using historical idioms. For example, many books aimed at the music teacher in the elementary school display little concern for aesthetic values or for educating children in the artistic thoughts of those composers whose reputation is established beyond doubt. Activities suggested too often involved acquiring behavior habits of performing in response to written symbols for some rather unmusical and uninspiringly simple versions of so called folk tunes. The performing, listening, and responding to notations tend to be predominantly concerned with an uneasy mixture of pentatonic tunes and simple tonal melodies of an idealised and stylistically neutral tonality. Many resemble nothing that existed in the practices of music of the past, either indigenous or art music. Even the pentatonic tunes and rhythms of the Kodaly and Orff school music schemes owe a great deal to this concept of stylistically neutral music, particularly in the English and American versions.

Thus there is little evidence of awareness of historical musical styles or the crucial importance of stylistic context to judge from the content of music programs that seek to promote literacy, yet they concentrate on a literacy that is historical. There is surely no such thing as historical music devoid of style and a specific cultural milieu. Misunderstandings about the crucial importance of varying cultural values abound.

In one book an elementary school music is the following:

> Let's walk down another corridor. We hear the music of Aida. Not surprising since the sixth grade classrooms are located here, and Aida correlates so nicely with the sixth grade social studies curriculum. (Raebeck and Wheeler, 1981a)

The writer does not go on to specify what the social studies actually are, but let us imagine that they involve a project on Egypt. What could be more natural for the teacher than to search for some music that is "Egyptian"? Too often the teacher will look to Western music rather than the ethnic culture of the region. Assumptions concerning musical meaning, superiority, and relevance of Western music are implicit. A basic one here is that because Verdi wrote an opera with an Egyptian story and characters then the music must, *de facto*, be "Egyptian." In fact, Verdi wrote "Italian" music in all his operas, and he would probably have written the same or similar music if the story had been set in Ancient Greece or modern Tokyo. To assume that the music is some sort of equivalent in its own right of the historical setting in ancient Egypt and of the story line begs all sorts of questions about musical meaning. Music can have meaning only by association. It is a nineteenth century concept that music has meaning of the kind assumed, and such practices are reflections of nineteenth century values. Children in today's world are influenced by quite different aesthetic standards and functions, and theories about cultural superiority are discredited, if not dead.

Yet, few are those adults, it seems, who can enjoy variously the merits of the most sophisticated chamber music recital as well as the Mills Brothers, Police, Charlie Parker, heavy rock, the electronic avant-garde, and grand opera. A hierarchy of quality involving notions of standards and taste linked with class, age, and life-style exists in the minds of many people, where chamber music and opera would be at the top. This attitude is reflected in music education in schools and is fed by tertiary institutions whose output is primarily concerned with historical skills and concepts in music. Inevitably there are implications of restrictions upon the contemporary from those who hold up values obtained from the "fossilised." From this point of view, and even more restrictive for the contemporary scene, is the notion that music of the past can actually live in its own future as a relevant entity with and to that future. Scholarly interest in the past is one thing, but to confuse this with the vitality of a living art form is another. The utterly laudable modern tendency to re-create historical music is regarded by many as a genuinely contemporary art form.

It is indeed a sophisticated mind that can easily re-create the spontaneity and immediacy of the "here and now" in expressions created in a different, not to mention dead, cultural milieu. In dealing with children it must be borne in mind that immediacy of impact and relevance to their immediate present are of vital importance in their perceptual processes. They do not possess such sophisticated mechanisms for introspection and metacognition as do adults, and relating to a past culture is for them (even more than for adults) a difficult process, particularly if they are required to respond to the immediacy of the impact of sound in this manner without either some immersion in the past or aids to more comprehensive under-standing from visual and other media. Yet, confusingly, they easily relate to nineteenth century musical idioms while watching films such as *The Empire Strikes Back* and *E. T.*

Is the aim of general music education for the nonperformer to de-velop the kind of sophistication referred to? If so, why? Is it to aid in producing sophisticated minds per se? In which case is music the best vehicle? Is it to preserve a cultural heritage that needs a certain type of sophistication as a product of training? What should be the role of high art of the past in a general musical education for all chil-dren? To judge from many practices in schools it is apparent that these questions have never been discussed adequately.

Music that forms a part of the normal day-to-day routine of a child's existency has special meaning to him, however tasteless or primitive it may appear to sophisticated adults. If this is ignored, then the music teacher is left with something like a Pygmalion syn-drome as a guiding ethos for his work. Some explanation of the pre-dominance of historical musical idioms found in schools is necessary, even though much of it is characterized as weak and neutral stylisti-cally and is no way comparable for the child to the background mu-sic he knows and appreciates from the films mentioned.

There is a school of thought that tends to the view eighteenth cen-tury tonality as the highest achievement of musical art, and by im-plication all that went before led up to it and what has followed contains many aberrations. Such a view is not purely musical in its origins. There are social and political reasons behind it. The rise of tonality coincided with the desire to escape from the "overcomplex" counterpoint by various religious/political movements during the Reformation and the Counter-Reformation. It led, however, to the development of a much simpler type of texture (melody and sup-porting harmony) in which the words could retain their impact on the singer and listener. By the eighteenth century harmonic theories had been advanced to a point of clarity and effectiveness of execu-tion in the works of composers such as Alberti and Pergolesi, not to mention Handel, Rameau, Vivaldi, and others. The church of non-conformity was quick to realise that singing was a vital aid in reli-gious experience, and during the eighteenth century the simplicity of the new tonality gave church leaders just the right kind of musical material to promote involvement of the masses in singing religious songs. The movement grew to enormous proportions so that by the nineteenth century large sectors of the populations of both Western Europe and North America had experienced mass choral religious music. So became established a mass belief in an inextricable link between tonal music and religion. In turn this became translated into a belief concerning quality, where simple tonal music is held up as the standard for questions of taste and aesthetic judgement against which other types of music are to be assessed. Modern education, with such powerful religious links because of its eighteenth and nineteenth century origins, has remained peculiarly conservative and restrictive in its attitude to music in schools.

Other classroom subjects seem not to have suffered the same kind of restriction and censure towards the use of twentieth century ideas as has music. Clearly the reasons have to do with the inbuilt conservatism referred to earlier, but predominantly with the immensely powerful impact on society of the educational movements in the eighteenth and nineteenth centuries that linked simple tonal music with religious experience and practices and linked religious teaching through music with basic educational aims and strategies. So emerged a tradition of rather colourless and stylistically neutral "school" music.

A sense of conflict is evident today between these old practices and values, as they linger on in education, and the effect of the laws of change and decay to which any society or individual is subject. Although we are going through a century of violent and rapid change reflected by practitioners in all arts, music education tends to remain historically rooted.

Of some relevance to the question of taste and aesthetic judgement is that of setting. For example, if we could fit the New York Philharmonic Orchestra or the London Symphony Orchestra into a public lavatory, would their performance have any impact on the musical appreciation of the respective audiences of the two orchestras if they performed there instead of the Lincoln Center or Royal Festival Hall? The chances are that it would have a severe impact on the financial state of each orchestra, for people like to have an appropriate setting for hearing the music usually associated with such orchestras. Similarly the usual audience for a heavy metal gig would feel somewhat out of place if it were held in the cathedral of St. John the Divine, New York, or Westminster Abbey, London. Not only would such settings seem inappropriate, but they might prove inhibiting factors affecting the enjoyment of such concerts, since conventions of location, dress, behavior, and even language become part of the whole experience in various modes of musical expression. A rock devotee would not talk about things such as intonation and balance and neither would a classical concert goer scream and wave his arms at the conductor during a performance, unless it was extremely bad!

From this perspective there is more to musical experience than the mere sound, and the problem for the music teacher is that he or she has to try to create a musical experience in a situation that is neither a concert hall, a cathedral, nor an open-air venue complete with an amplification system and stage. Thus we can identify certain types of music with certain buildings or locations, but what kind of music is associated with the school and classroom? Can other types of music be easily transplanted there to advantage? When a setting such as St. Mark's, Venice, is a kind of musician's "studio" for composers such as the Gabrielis, or Monteverdi, can their music, composed for that building and its acoustic properties, be satisfactorily transplanted to a tiny chapel on a Welsh hillside? Isn't it the case that the latter has its own musical tradition rooted in its culture and the type of building and beliefs of the populace surrounding it, just as the former has its traditions shaped by forces that emanate from its distinctly different building and populace? It would certainly reflect some kind of hypocrisy in school music if it were said simply that music is music wherever it is played. Perhaps this has some relevance to the charge made above that much of the music children are given in school is lacking in style. Clearly if there is difficulty identifying what sort of a musical venue a classroom is then is it not surprising that the music practised there tends to be neutral and stylistically vague.

Music education is thus seen to be very much at the mercy of its origins and close links with religious instruction and experience. In fact, the popular view of musical taste and standards is also linked with the religious use made of music during the last few centuries.

While the schools retained a close link with the churches an underlying ethos for the whole educative process could be tacitly understood, and music was always the bridge that linked the two. Thus music had not so much an educative function as a social or a political one. Since the power and influence of the church has diminished in education schools have identified other purposes than the nineteenth century one of leading children along the pathway to God through music and literacy. Unfortunately this has left music somewhat high and dry in the sense that no clear alternative function to that referred to has been satisfactorily assigned it. The consequence of this is that general class music lessons tend to have inadequate purposes and aims. Gone is the motivating force in using them for hymn singing, or similar religious activity, and the teacher is left with little else than introducing children to musical literacy using so-called children's music, the artistic and aesthetic quality of which is sometimes difficult to detect. In fact accusations of triviality and unsuitability in terms of intellectual challenge are invited by many of the song collections and methods used in the general music lesson. God is gone, and by default we are left with literacy alone.

2

AESTHETIC ISSUES IN MUSIC

> Music is one of the ways in which man's nature expresses itself, and it is sometimes so closely bound up with human existence that a discussion of it cannot possibly be regarded as irrelevant to the history of mankind.
>
> Jack Westrup: *Introduction to Musical History*

MUSIC should not be regarded as a universal language so much as a universal phenomenon that manifests itself in many different ways as a product of its cultural environment. Viewed in this way there are certain difficulties apparent if one attempts to make value judgements concerning the meaning of music from different cultural environments and meaning is often tied up with notions of quality.

Value judgements in music are concerned with aesthetic awareness, and the precise nature of this has been the subject of philosophical debate from ancient times to the present. Moreover, the various viewpoints that have emerged reflect changing fashions in modes of thought rather than progress towards a certain truth.

From the time of Plato onwards man has been concerned with the nature of beauty as a subject of philosophical discourse. Without this there tends to be merely an apprehension of the object or event of beauty rather than a discussion as to what constituted beauty and why. Certainly aesthetic awareness is related to the impact of an object or event on our perceptions in terms of how it affects our "feelings." The word *feelings* has to do with emotional as well as intellectual functioning. The problem with the value judgement, however, is that it tends to be individual and highly personal, therefore highly subjective; along with this have grown notions of serious and nonserious music, with their corollary more important and less important. On the other hand, there seems less evidence of the existence of music critics or historians in the musical life of various primitive cultures. The emphasis is on the integral role of music in the day-to-day lives of such people. In primitive societies music had a different purpose and effect. Marius Schneider explains something of this:

> Every human being has his own sound, or is a particular melody. To stop a magician from imitating this melody and so getting its bearer into his power, primitive man thinks it necessary to keep his own melody as secret from sorcerers as his "real" name. (Wellesz, 1969, p.10)

This concerns totemistic music and its inextricable links between life, belief in magical powers, and the music, as well as the significance these elements had in influencing man's behaviour. His basic survival instinct was affected by such beliefs and suggests a rather more ominous function for music than exists in today's complex Western society. It does not, however, suggest value judgements of the kind we have grown used to today. Rather it suggests that music was such a vital and integral part of existence, concerning both life and afterlife, that its auditory content, and therefore the elements lending themselves to modern aesthetic value judgements, had little significance without its function.

Value judgements of anything have to take account of how effectively the evaluated object performs its accepted function. There seems little evidence that primitive man was able to change his sound or melody if he found it not performing to his liking, since he was born with it. He was, as it were, stuck with it through life, and death in some cultures, and had not the modern advantage of being able to go down to the nearest music shop to get a different one. This emphasizes how seriously primitive man regarded his particular sound or melody. To him it was rather like an arm or leg. How different is our modern view of music and its function in our lives!

Radocy and Boyle (1979) indicate ten major functions of music ranging from emotional expression, aesthetic enjoyment, and entertainment to those activities which are subject to social and political pressures or accepted norms in terms of value, such as religious and ceremonial functions. The authors state that "music appears to serve essentially the same functions in most cultures" (p. 164): Our lives tend to be broken up into different states of mental activity and awareness, play and work for example, and these, being common to mankind everywhere, generate musical activities. Thus there would be similar situations in all cultures where music would be used, but there would not be, for example, universal views on the importance of music as a potentially lethal force in our lives. Whereas primitive man regarded music as something as personal and vital as his body, modern man regards it as something to be evaluated in terms of its effects on him.

What is intriguing is the possibility of primitive man displaying aesthetic awareness. There is little doubt concerning the seriousness with which totemistic societies regarded music. According to Schneider, "they even hold 'nature' concerts in which each singer imitates a particular sound (waves, wind, groaning trees, cries of frightened animals), 'concerts' of surprising magnificence and beauty" (Wellesz, 1969, p. 9). Whether the beauty was merely in the eyes of the beholder or also appreciated by the performers is not made clear. Radocy and Boyle (1979) maintain, however, that "the creating and contemplating of beauty in music is evident in Western culture as well as many other major cultures including those of China, Japan, Arabia, India, and Indonesia" (p. 165).

Presumably we can only speculate as to whether what we call aesthetic awareness was evident in more primitive societies. There is certainly a great deal of evidence in the literature of ancient civilizations of a highly developed aesthetic awareness that even has relevance to us today. For example, the Old Testament Psalms are full of literary evidence of a highly developed set of values concerning "feelings," aesthetic awareness of the ways in which objects, events, or the memories evoked by them affect the observer's emotional stability. "By the waters of Babylon we sat down and wept when we remembered thee 0 Zion" is but one illustration from Psalm 137.

What is different today seems to be the concept of quality as applied to different types of musical practices. At least as early as the seventeenth century one can find qualitative statements concerning the relative values of some types of music as compared with others. One has to look no further than the diaries and other writings of various English wits of the seventeenth century to find them.

Judgements concerning music are necessarily so subjective it is not easy to prove satisfactorily that, for example, a Beethoven symphony is a more valuable and worthwhile piece of music than the totemistic music of an aboriginal. Neither is it much easier to prove scientifically that one Beethoven symphony is better than another. Nevertheless many value judgements of this type are made, and some even think it an important element in critical study. Westrup (1967) outlines something of the problem in his discussion on the scope of musical history in Western culture:

> It is the business of a historian to be critical . . . it is not sufficient for him to record facts, he must also judge their relative importance. In the case of music this involves a judgement of values [but] this opinion of the historian's function is not universally held. It is often maintained that appreciation of the values of music is irrelevant. (p. 15)

He goes on to say that without such appreciation commentary on music would be "arid deserts of scientific record" (p. 16) and that "the exaggerations to which enthusiasm may lead are insignificant beside the futility of an approach which refuses to recognize aesthetic satisfaction as a spur to judgement" (p. 16).

The power to affect people in a way that induces aesthetic satisfaction is held up as significant in judgements on music. If one could now define aesthetic satisfaction in such a way as to conform to all circumstances of its manifestations, then judgements on music would be relatively easy to justify by this criterion. The problem still remains, however, that different types of music affect different people in different ways. Even the same people are affected differently by the same piece of music at different times in their lives. This is not to deny the power of music but rather to emphasize its elusive and somewhat contradictory nature. Neither is it an attempt to refute the values that now obtain in Western culture; exposure of associated difficulties is more the aim.

Davies (1978) states that

> music does not really satisfy the requirements that would completely

> justify its being called a "language" . . . music seems to have something
> in common with simple forms of sensory experience like warmth, taste,
> or the smell of jacket-baked potatoes. (p. 25).

On the other hand, a number of writers have produced books demonstrating the nature of music's language. Some attribute quite specific meanings to certain musical phenomena, depending upon context and expectation, e.g. Cooke (1959).

Davies goes on to say that

> music is something of a mystery . . . [and] does not appear to pass on any
> message we can readily identify . . . Despite these elusive qualities, people
> in all parts of the world indulge in musical pursuits with great enthusiasm,
> and their lives are often profoundly affected as a result. (p. 25).

We have then an art form that is universally practised, has power to affect people in many different ways, often profoundly, is manifest in many different forms, yet is so elusive that it apparently defies enquiry as to the precise nature of the qualities that generate these effects. Even Davies in his avowedly "objective" examination of the nature of musical phenomena merely asks the question "Might there not be certain tonal configurations which have certain physiognomic properties?" (p. 105). He cites no evidence for their proven existence, but neither can he subscribe to the view that certain visual configurations have physiognomic properties that contain intrinsic meanings for the perceiver.

We know from experience that certain types of tunes and harmonies can excite certain types of emotions in a certain type of listener. Patriotic tunes or hymns generate patriotic feelings, love songs generate tender passions, sporting songs or chants generate sentiments of support for one's favourite team, religious music of a solemn kind generates suitably solemn feelings, and so on. These are evidence of associations of sociocultural origin formed with certain types of musical expressions. Are they in fact evidence for intrinsic meaning in the musical sounds?

The word *intrinsic* is defined as relating to something that belongs naturally, or exists within, not coming from the outside (*Oxford Advanced Learner's Dictionary*). Thus the question relates to whether or not the "natural" properties of musical sounds contain elements such as patriotism, love, or religion, which do not have to be imposed by but are self-evident to the listener.

In answer, it must be concluded from available evidence that such instrinsic elements cannot be attributed to any musical phenomena. Therefore, all interpretations of music have to be learned through association of meanings with sounds. There is in fact strong support for such a theory of musical meaning. Even during the nineteenth century, when many gave credence to the then current belief that certain musical sounds possessed certain identifiable meanings related to nonmusical events, there was by no means a completely united attitude, and there was evidence then of belief in associated rather than intrinsic meanings. The most famous opponent of intrinsic meaning was Eduard Hanslick, a Viennese music critic. In 1854 his book *The Beautiful in Music* appeared, in which he virtually demolished arguments for the view that music can have the kind of intrinsic meaning that was claimed by many composers of his day, notably Wagner. However, he wrote the following on the effects of music on our feelings (Hanslick, 1957):

> Though all arts without exception have power to act on our feelings, yet the mode in which music displays it is, undoubtedly, peculiar to this art. Music operates on our emotional faculty with greater intensity and rapidity than the product of any art. A few chords may give rise to a frame of mind which a poem can induce only by lengthy exposition, or a picture by prolonged contemplation. (p. 67).

The stronger initial impact of auditory stimulation, compared with visual, as it affects the perceptual processes is what Hanslick is referring to. We are interested, however, in whether or not we can perceive sadness, for example, in a melody because of the intrinsic acoustic properties of the melody. Hanslick says, "It is, aesthetically, quite correct to speak of a theme as having sad or noble accent, but not as expressing the sad or noble feelings of the composer" (p. 74).

If musical sounds are able to evoke emotion then there must be some identifiable acoustic characteristic that does the evoking. Looking further at Hanslick's views we find he is clearly sceptical about the power of musical characteristics to excite specifically intended meanings. He refers to "those inherently fallacious precepts for the excitation of definite emotions by musical means" (p. 87). Earlier in his book he describes some of Handel's self-borrowings, clearly citing them as evidence against the notion that music can have intrinsic meaning: "Winterfield has shown that many of the

most celebrated airs from the *Messiah,* including those most of all ad-
mired as being especially suggestive of piety were taken from secular
duets (mostly erotic)" (p. 35). Obviously he is arguing that if the music had erotic meaning in its earlier context how can it be said to
have religious meaning in a later one if there were intrinsic meanings inherent in the acoustic phenomena!

Other writers on music and meanings have expressed similar
doubts about the power of music to excite specific feelings, particularly if it is claimed that this power stems entirely from the musical
material and not from the imposed meaning from the listener. For
example, Leonard Meyer (1956) says that "many affective experiences attributed directly to musical stimuli may in point of fact be
the products of unconscious image processes" (p. 257). He also talks
of "connotations" (p. 258), which he defines as "associations which
are shared in common by a group of individuals." Richard Wollheim
(1968) puts it another way when he says that "we see or experience
emotion in a work of art; we do not read it off" (p. 76). The inward
state of the perceiver assumes importance for Wollheim:

> We think of a work of art as expressive in the sense in which a gesture or
> a cry would be expressive . . . alongside this notion is another, which we
> apply when we think of an object as expressive of a certain condition be-
> cause, when we are in that condition, it seems to match, or correspond
> with what we experience inwardly. (p. 47).

The characteristics that appear to match such inward states are only
expressive of generalities, however, particularly in the case of music,
as Schopenhauer, cited by Pratt (1968), explains:

> Music stands alone, it is cut off from all other arts. It does not express a
> particular and definite joy, sorrow, anguish, delight or mood of peace,
> but joy, sorrow, anguish, delight, peace of mind in themselves, in the
> abstract, in their essential nature, without accessories and therefore
> without their customary motives. Yet it enables us to grasp and share
> them in their full quintessence. (p. vii).

The theme is quite clear. The writers previously quoted display a
remarkable uniformity of viewpoint, and it can be deduced from this
particular body of opinion that music does not have intrinsic meaning concerning moods, or attitudes of mind, but that it is perfectly
possible for the listener to attribute such meanings to musical
sounds. In this case the meaning would match an inner state of the

listener, or put another way, the characteristics of the musical sounds would lend themselves to the kind of associations that would enable a listener to match their physical characteristics with his or her state of mind.

It can be said, however, that although it is difficult to accept that particular chords or melodic sequences have intrinsic meaning that relate moods or other feelings to be read off as it were by the listener, it must be the case that certain chords or melodic phrases have certain acoustic properties that lend themselves to the kind of associations referred to. Thus, although one cannot read pathos in a minor rather than a major melody, it is possible to apply pathos to particular melodies because of their shape and use of pitch. This meaning can be transmitted to others who are then able to perceive it by association. As Davies (1978) has pointed out, it is not that a major tune has particularly happy characteristics because it is major nor that a minor tune has sad ones because it is minor. He cites two particularly sad tunes, both in a major key, to illustrate this: the hymn "For Those in Peril on the Sea" and the "extremely miserable" song "Che faro senza Euridice" from Gluck's *Orfeo* (p. 103).

Many composers have shown that it is necessary to have some kind of collateral information to perceive intended meanings from their music. Berlioz (*see* Arts Council, 1969) wrote a lengthy "programme note" for the first performance of his *Fantastic* Symphony in 1845, in which he said, "In concerts in which this symphony is performed, the distribution of this programme to the audience is vital for the complete understanding of the work" (p. 57)

Stravinsky (*see* White, 1966) would only go as far as to suggest that his *Symphony in Three Movements* is inspired by a documentary film of "scorched earth tactics in China" and added that it was possible to find in it "traces of impressions and experiences coloured by this our arduous time of sharp and shifting events, of despair and hope, of continual torments, of tension, and at last a cessation and relief" (p. 391)

Since it is difficult to find evidence that musical sounds contain intrinsic properties that give them meanings of the kind referred to, it must be concluded that so far as present knowledge extends, such meanings applied to music are a result of social conditions and cultural influences within the cultural milieu. They are in fact a product of the cultural impact on the organising capacities of the human brain as it responds to the sensory input effected by physical characteristics of the sound we call music.

Although one might be able to claim a certain amount of similarity of musical materials from one cultural milieu to another, particularly in the history of Western art music, this does not aid in understanding their different use in different milieux. Westrup (1967) explains that "the history of art-forms is rooted in social conditions" (p. 69).
He also states that

> there is no single, universal cause which brings music to birth: the factors are many and varied. They may include the demands of an accepted religion, the vanity of a patron, the pride of a community or the rebellion of an individual. (p. 68)

Lomax, cited by Radocy and Boyle (1979), puts it differently:

> Music is man's vehicle for expressing what is most basic in his relationships with others . . . [it] reflects and reinforces the kinds of behaviour essential to its main subsistence efforts and to its central and controlling social institution. (p. 177)

In the chapter "Music as a Phenomenon of Man," they conclude that

> many musicologists and music historians concerned with the development of music in traditional Western culture also recognize music as a sociocultural force which must be studied within its societal and cultural framework. (p. 178)

This begs many questions concerning the educational use of music. If, as has been pointed out, many scholars subscribe to the view that music must be studied within its sociocultural framework, what do we expect of children when we present historical music for them to play or listen to? The answer must be concerned with the circumstances in which such music is presented. For example, in the cathedral choir schools of Europe, historical music seems the most obvious type of music to expect, largely because of the purpose of such schools in maintaining religious worship. The history of much Western music is bound up with the history and development of religious worship. Similarly, in a youth orchestra it would be unthinkable not to play historical music because of the historical origins and repertoire of the orchestra. Certainly children attending a madrigal choir would also expect to sing historical music, and presumably their interest in music lies in this historical field. These are examples of modern day special interest groups, where the historical bias of the activity is expected, even relished. What can be considered suitable for the general music education of the masses of children who have not developed such sophisticated tastes and whose opinions are subject to the vagueries of their social and aesthetic upbringing? The music teacher in a classroom has to select some kind of musical activity. If it is historical then there must be some background supplied. Even if it is contemporary there is no guarantee that the conditions under which the child developed are the same as, or similar to, those which produced the music. This is not to say that music is a communication that cannot reach those outside the environment that nurtured it, but rather than this is an important factor that has tended to be ignored on the assumption that the language of music, rather than the practice of music, is a universal phenomenon.

An important question facing the music teacher, therefore, concerns choice of material and the conventions surrounding that material. For example, should one teach music as high art, as a form of amusement, as an adjunct to ritual? Should one teach the musical idioms of jazz (traditional or modern?), eighteenth century tonality, the electronic or percussion avant-garde, various types of "pop," ethnic music, etc.? What about the customs that surround each type; does one teach those as well? Even if the choice made favours tonal music, for example, there is a great deal of variety within that broad description. Tonal music embraces styles as varied as the "American" idioms of Gershwin, Glen Miller, Cole Porter, or Henry Mancini, and the "English" idioms of Vaughan Williams, Holst, or Elgar, as well as the "Viennese" idioms of Mozart, Haydn, Beethoven, or Schubert. Further discussion in the following chapters will attempt to illuminate the nature of historical and contemporary practices in music and education from other perspectives so as to aid the process of clarification of aims and suitability of musical education in the general classroom. From this chapter it is argued that there are no universals in terms of meaning in music that can be applied to any single style or musical practice and that values associated with any type of music have to be learned. Of course, this is not to suggest that they should not be taught. The implication is more insidious: Because of the belief in a lingua franca of music (tonal music) and in universal values there follows the dangerous assumption that simple, neutral tonal music can be relevant to artistic practices that are culture bound, and "universal" values do not need to be taught because they are "universal."

3

MUSIC EDUCATION IN MODERN HISTORY
Religion, Social Training, and Good Taste

In the history of Western civilization the significance of the role of the Christian Church cannot be overstressed. Until fairly recently the church was a dominating force in all aspects of life in Western Europe. One important facet of the church's function was, and still is, to foster religious worship involving the mass of the people in ceremonies performed by the priests. A most significant feature of such ceremonies is music in many functions ranging from those of mass participation to those of specialist performance by a select few. For these reasons the history of music, and everything associated with it in recent history, is inextricably bound up with the history of the church. As changes occurred in religious worship, due to various political or social factors, so changes occurred in the scope, form, and function of musicians employed by the church — the most important employer of musicians in the last thousand years.

Religious Origins of Music Education

The earliest attempts at education in Western civilization were those of the church, and the earliest forms of music education were those designed to serve the needs of the church. These needs were, predominantly, singing religious texts in various styles. Guido d'Arezzo, a Benedictine monk born in Paris circa 995, developed the first visual aids to learning pitch notations, and therefore pitch movements, in music education. Whether he invented or merely perfected them is not known. He took the hexachord (the first 6 notes of the major scale) as a basis, developed the application of its movements to the physiognomy of the hand (known as the Guidonian Hand), and used this and the gamut as teaching devices for sight singing. These were in use from the time Guido introduced them in the eleventh century to at least the seventeenth or eighteenth century in Europe. By the sixteenth century knowing the gamut was something of a *sine qua non* for those educated formally. Incidentally, in the seventeenth century there was a mounting chorus of criticism against the excessive complication of the gamut and its increasing irrelevance for music of the day. Rainbow (1967) quotes a number of such instances, including R. Midgley's comment that the gamut was a "long bead-role of hard and useless names" (p. 14) and that of Roger North, who observed that as far as children were concerned, they must endure the "soured and mysterious Gamut, which they must rehearse antrorsum and retrorsum while understanding nothing of its significance, [and which] should be supplanted by something simpler" (p. 15).

The original purposes of such musical education were entirely religious. Music was taught exclusively for the purpose of training men and boys to perform in religious ritual. Although the secularisation of society gathered momentum during the sixteenth century and music was taught as part of a general education rather than purely for religious use, there followed movements for establishing mass education in the eighteenth and nineteenth centuries that were religious in content and aims. In these mass movements in England and elsewhere music was a most important feature, for it was felt that through music the masses could be made more morally aware in their behaviour. Bishop Porteous of London in 1790 wrote:

> When it is considered that there are now three hundred thousand Sunday School children in varous parts of the kingdom, if one third of them can be taught to perform the psalm tunes tolerably well, these useful institutions will contribute no less to the improvement of parochial psalmody than to the reformation of the lower orders of the people.

(Rainbow, 1967, p. 20)

Thus he makes clear that music could be made to serve a specific social purpose in the movement of religious revival that was taking place through the growth of education for the masses. The kind of songs that little children had to sing were full of indoctrination and intimidation, as the following nineteenth century songs demonstrate:

Song 11 There is a dreadful hell, and everlasting pains! Where sinners must with devils dwell, in Darkness, fire and chains.

Song 13 'Tis dangerous to provoke a God! His pow'r and vengeance none can tell;
One stroke of his almighty rod shall send young sinners quick to hell. (Rainbow 1967, p. 36)

By way of contrast, the following, from the Harrow School Songs, pointed the young children of the wealthy in different directions:

God give us bases to guard or beleaguer,
Games to play out whether earnest or fun;
Fights for the fearless and goals for the eager,
Twenty and thirty and forty years on.

The 19th century saw some protestations that music in mass education should serve different functions than those of mere religious indoctrination. W.E. Hickson, in the preface to *The Singing Master* of 1836, wrote the following:

It is a great error in any system of education provided for the children of the poor to conclude that it is no part of the duty of an instructor to teach the means of rational enjoyment. (Rainbow 1967, p. 40)

Although Hickson's was one of a number of voices echoing similar sentiments, the power and influence of the church remained to dominate mass musical education content throughout the nineteenth century. Thus generation after generation had their musical tastes formed in such a manner. Moreover, in England at any rate, music was frowned upon in some quarters as a frivolous and useless occupation. In the eighteenth century the powerful Lord Chesterfield made one of the most influential statements in this respect when he warned his son about the "hazardous charms of music" (Rainbow

1967, p. 25). Even earlier, the philosoper John Locke did not exactly fire his readers with enthusiasm about the values of music in his 1692 essay "Some Thoughts Concerning Education," when he wrote:

> Music . . . wastes so much of a young man's time to gain but a moderate skill in it; and engages often in such odd company that many think it better spared . . . amongst all those things that ever came into the List of Accomplishments, I think I may give it last place. (Rainbow 1967, p. 24)

Such a raw philistinism was not found on the continent to the same degree, and countries like Switzerland, Germany, and Austria (or their constituent states, as they then were) used music in their general education programmes in a way that was the envy of many in England like Hickson. Without doubt England was the home of a monumental musical philistinism that was to have repercussions in the mass music education of the nineteenth and even the twentieth centuries. One of the effects was to make music somehow synonymous with sin in the eyes of the populace, and only through its use in religious purposes could it therefore be redeemed. Such ideas spread to North America, as well as to other parts of the globe where British influence could be found. Unfortunately, one of the most troublesome outcomes for future generations was that concerning the aesthetics of music. Bound up with judgements about music was religious feeling and the role of music in engendering it.

The Rise of a Secular Musical Education

The development of tonal music coincided with the rise of mass education of a predominantly religious nature, and it is interesting to see how values in tonal music become a paradigm for all musical quality for the wrong reasons. People felt, naturally enough, that since tonal music had the seal of approval of the church then it would have universal approval because the church was felt to represent omnipotence. There were few musicians in the past who had nothing at all to do with the church, either writing music for it or performing in its ritual. So developed a tight and enclosed circle of influence whereby religion, musical taste, and music's function became inextricably bound up together in the minds of people.

Nevertheless, music did serve different purposes, but they tended to reflect the various social strata and life-styles of society. For example, Hickson's plea for music to be used as a means of "rational enjoyment" was not entirely a plea for the working classes to be allowed to enjoy music in the manner of European aristocracy. Ideas of "rational enjoyment" for the "lower orders" in England did not extend much beyond singing good and moral songs for the betterment of mind, body, and soul. To be fair, Hickson was echoing some slightly more hedonistic European notions when he qualified "enjoyment" as "a moment's relaxation . . . to relieve the montony of . . . existence by some pleasurable excitement" (Rainbow 1967, p. 40).

The wealthy classes of Europe had enjoyment music for its own sake, or other nonreligious reasons, for hundreds of years. It took a lot of convincing in England that such was for the "lower orders." It must also be pointed out that the mainstream of artistic musical activity in Europe from the late sixteenth century onwards began to develop outside the church, whatever the denomination. The effect of the Reformation and Counter-Reformation on musicians was to diminish to some extent the artistic freedom they had hitherto enjoyed. As music became more and more subject to the demands of political and social pressures inside the church, musicians began to look outside for opportunities to explore their creative talents to the full. So developed opera, instrumental music, and all the major forms we now know. With the church relinquishing its role as the prime patron and instigator of musical activity and development, the musicians turned to the rising power of the aristocratic ruler as a source of artistic employment. This meant a growth in secular instrumental music for entertainment. In turn it meant work for instrumental teachers, instrument makers, and musical directors, as well as performers and composers. Singing was still regarded as the major form of music making however, because of its historical role in church ritual. So when, during the seventeenth and eighteenth centuries, books began to appear offering schemes for learning various instruments, the singing voice tended to have pride of place, thus reinforcing the notion that all musicianship stems from the ability to sing. There was not any firm evidence for this, of course; it was merely a matter of paying homage to a great and glorious past when vocal music served the church's need and was king of music.

In terms of teaching, many books offered a kind of "you can do it too" programme by selling music instruction as something to make performance accessible to all, provided the individual was willing to work hard enough. For example, in 1737 Peter Prelleur published the *Modern Music Master* and in the preface explains:

> Music has been always esteemed one of the most agreeable and Rational Diversions Mankind could be blest with, and is now become so general throughout the great part of Europe that almost everyone is a judge of Fine Ayre and True Harmony. But as its worth has given it a place among the liberal sciences, it is like the rest of them to be attained only by study and practice.

He does not go on to define criteria for judgements, but he does indicate the extent of the growth of secular music, even if one might disagree that it was open to "everyone" as he implies. In notes to the facsimile edition of the *Modern Music Master,* Alexander Hyatt King states that "Prelleur's book was a compendium which reflected all the most popular aspects of music making in his age, with a little theory thrown in for good measure." The six sections of the book deal with singing (placed first), flute, German flute, oboe, violin, and harpsichord. Each section contains hints on how to play the instrument and includes scales, pieces, and general notes on its history, as well as rules about various ways of ornamenting. This reflects that music making was a feature of life in some circles in London at the time despite the philistinism generated by Locke and Lord Chesterfield.

We have, then, a picture of two basic types of music education and, therefore, musical experience during the eighteenth century. There is indicated a clear distinction between music for the lower orders and music for those with title, power, or wealth. The former was seen as pedagogic in aiding the processes of reformation of character and control of behaviour, whereas the latter was regarded as entertainment, diversion, or an object of aesthetic value. This dichotomy lingered strongly in the nineteenth century through the rise of the new industrial classes with all the associated social and political problems of expanding urban communities. Hickson's plea for music to be concerned with "rational enjoyment" was a reflection of the revolutionary ideas of his times, which eventually gave birth to modern socialism in all its manifestations. Just as people were beginning to show interest in social structures and the concept of equality, so were musicians and writers beginning to question the function and meaning of music as an art form and as an influence in life generally. The power of music to "soothe the savage breast" was well known and generally believed. With the rise to prominence of new social issues this "power" was available for harnessing in the interests of those with authority to manipulate. So, during the nineteenth century, the moralising purposes behind public development, such as mass education, had their effect on attitudes towards music — it was to be used as much for "soothing" the "savage" worker as anything. This reforming role for music, identified by the Bishop of London in 1790, was to become significant in defining aims for music education.

Concepts of Taste and Quality

Just as the rise of tonality coincided with the beginnings of mass education in modern society, so did it coincide with the earliest modern statements, and developing interests, concerning musical meaning and aesthetic judgements. Since tonal music and its artistic use were the focus of such value judgements, there is now a well-established body of comment that has assumed something of the aura of holy writ with tonal music the holy object. In trying to establish aesthetic values in music today there is a natural tendency to start with these judgements on historical music. The problem for the music educator concerns the wisdom of applying historical value judgements to contemporary music. With such a background of religious, social, and political change during the last few hundred years can it be accepted that aesthetic values in music remain constant and are not subject to the influence of such change or that the criteria established concerning tonal music of the past are still valid with respect to music produced in response to conditions that now exist? Do notions of good taste from a past era carry much relevance for today's educator? From the writings of musicians and philosophers of the past we can get some idea of the nature of the value judgements that were formed, and this is necessary before attempting to answer such questions.

The concept of good taste carries some weight in the view of those who have the task of managing society. This is particularly so in the case of the arts, if only because of the absence of measuring and assessment techniques of a more objective nature. The historical origin of concepts of good taste can explain some attitudes that prevail today and can perhaps contribute to a more objective analysis of the role and function of music in education. Some of today's concepts of good taste are bound up with the eighteenth century avant-garde of composers who strove for harmonic and melodic (therefore, tonal) simplicity. The mid-eighteenth century avant-garde associated its compositional techniques with ideas of simplification in contrast to the complexities of the baroque composers of the previous generation. As Lawrence (1978) explains, "the reasons put forward for this simplification are commonplace enough: in order to convey 'feeling' more directly, simpler compositional techniques must be employed" (p. 162).

Further, as Lawrence points out, the desire to express oneself more clearly has been common in the development of music since the early seventeenth century. Along with it goes an accusation of lack of clarity for the previous generation of composers. The words of Gluck (1769), relating to his opera *Alceste*, explain the desire: "My most strenuous efforts must be directed in search of a noble simplicity, thus avoiding a parade of difficulty at the expense of clarity." Lawrence explains further:

> This whole process of simplification . . . became the "good taste" of the mid-eighteenth century, to which the essayists continually refer . . . Leopold Mozart wishes "to pave the way for music loving youth which will guide them with certainty to good taste in music," and there is continuous reference to what C.P.E. Bach calls "our present elegant taste." (p. 162)

Further, we read Leopold Mozart's statement that "taste and technique must run together from the start of a musician's education" (p. 162).

Thus the picture obtained is one whereby good taste is deemed to be commensurate with clarity. This is interpreted by Lawrence as implying clarity of tonal language in the use of harmony and melody. Clarity in this context means, therefore, clarity of key, phrase structure, and cadence, and this is the same as saying simplicity, for clarity and simplicity are meant to be synonymous for these eighteenth century composers. Examined in this fashion, it can be said that such ideas are the bedrock of what is known as classicism in music, where balance, proportion, and synthesis are the aspirations of composers. Such ideas of musical art were exemplified in the works of J. Haydn, W.A. Mozart, and their contemporaries in Vienna and surrounding areas. Since W.A. Mozart was educated musically to some extent by his father, Leopold, it is important to know what ideas lay behind the father's instruction. Concerning this we can deduce that the young Wolfgang Amadeus was brought up to display "taste and technique." At the same time it is necessary to acknowledge that other influences were at work that also are evident in the music of the classicists. The movement known as Sturm and Drang in German literature heralded the first conscious notions of what came to be known as romanticism. Lang (1941) explains how the two forces interacted:

> In Hegel, Schelling, and Schliermacher, classicism and romanticism met, in Beethoven classicism became romantic, and in Schubert romanticism became classic. The classicists in general often appeared romantically inclined in their youth and again in old age. (p. 746)

As Lang intimates, it is not strictly accurate to translate the romantic ideas of literature into those musical works which were contemporary or nearly so. Romanticism worked differently in music: "Romanticism was no longer an ideal . . . only an artistic metier" (p. 746).

The concept of good taste was not destroyed by romanticism in music. The argument became concerned with how effectively the composer could represent his ideas in music. Ideas of classical form and balance in music are not inimical to the ideas of romanticism. Passages in Mozart symphonies, for example, can be and often are described as "romantic" in mood, and Mendelssohn provided a perfect synthesis.

Schelling formulated certain principles of romanticism in his lecture "On the Relation of the Plastic Arts to Nature," delivered in Munich in 1807. In it he stated that "the principle of organic form, the specifically romantic principle . . . rests on one of the most fundamental distinctions known to philosophy . . . that between essence and existence" (Read 1968 p. 16).

The creative, intuitive power of the romantic artist acted as a mediator between essence, the realm of perfection, and existence, the realm of imperfect human acts. Thus to the romantic, art was the link between the two. This not new. In Plato's system we read of something similar. Lang explains how music is regarded in this respect:

> The philosopher sees an analogy between the movements of the soul and
> the musical progressions; therefore the aim of music cannot be amuse-
> ment but a harmonic education and perfection of the soul and the quiet-
> ing of passions. Consequently music is, to a certain degree, the most
> immediate expression of eros, a bridge between ideas and phenomena.
> (p. 13)

There are those who subscribe to the view that music has always performed this function and, therefore, has always been a "romantic expression" in this sense. Certainly Mendelssohn (1842) subscribed to this view when he wrote that the thoughts expressed by music are not too indefinite for words to convey but too definite. He felt music was far more effective than words could be in their fulfillment of the bridge function referred to by Lang.

These ideas bring us to the familiar nineteenth century beliefs in music as an art form capable of generating and expressing emotion. They are described as familiar so as to emphasize the contemporary universality of this concept.

It has already been pointed out that there was a difference between education of the "lower orders" in music and that of more privileged sectors of society. Recipients of the former were not made aware of contemporary views in the way the latter were. It is thus possible to see clearly the time lag that occurred between the "romantic" concept of music as it occurred in the practices of musicians and the experience of such by the mass of the public. In many instances this awareness by the general public came as late as this century, aided by the use of overtly sentimental music, plagiarised from the nineteenth century romantic composers, in the cinema. Similarly, concepts of "good taste" and "balance," appealing to the more dispassionate natures, became common knowledge only after the growth of education at the secondary and tertiary levels that occurred well into this century. Not only do the recipients of such education at higher levels have to cope with the explosion of knowledge about the past, but there is the present coexisting. The present reflects a much more complex set of attitudes and formative influences than anything that has occurred in the past. No sooner had present-day society come to grips with the complex ideas from central Europe concerning first classical balance and poise, then romantic concepts of art's links between "essence" and "existence" emanating from the eighteenth and nineteenth centuries, when it was noticed

that some musicians and other artists of the present day were practising radically different concepts of art.

Review

For the moment, however, it is necessary to clarify this description of both the ideas and the events that contributed to the formation of attitudes concerning music and music education during the
last 200 years.

First there is the role of the church in providing the main employment for musicians for such a long period. Inevitably this has influenced people into thinking that the most serious function of music
is in religious activity. Then there is the view that music somehow
"hath charms to soothe a savage breast, to soften rocks or bend a
knotted oak" (William Congreve, 1697). This gave rise to the use of
music as a civilizing force in the early days of mass education. In addition, those in authority saw in music a means of religious indoctrination of the masses of the "lower orders." All this coincided with
the rise of tonality and the relatively simple and therefore "tasteful"
melodies and harmonies, which were perfectly suited to mass participation. This in turn meant that simple tonal music became synonymous in many people's minds with order, the church, and discipline.
There coexisted the somewhat hedonistic life-styles of the aristocratic classes who saw music as a means to different ends, and to
whom tonal music was merely the latest development in one art that
was an integral part of their life-styles' diverse entertainments.

The rise of the music critic also coincided with the rise of tonality,
and since the writings on value judgments in music concern themselves with tonal music, there has developed a feeling that criteria for
assessing certain types of tonal music are also valid for all music. A
main contributory factor in this is that mass awareness and understanding of artistic endeavours tend to be retrospective and to trail
far behind activities of change and exploration by practising artists.

The legacy of all this is still with us, if only because of the inevitable time lag that occurred between the rise of ideas, their appearance
in practice, and their dissemination among the mass of the populace.
Even today, for example, it is by no means the case that mass education in music has ensured that everyone is familiar even with eighteenth century concepts of "classical" art, despite additional exposure

by the media. Thus there is a confused and nonsynchronous situation whereby attitudes and ideas emanating from the past are mixed with those of the present, and relevance to the contemporary becomes a major issue. Some of these influences are more potent than others. In the mass education movement, that of the church is paramount when it comes to music because of the historical religious and educational use of music. This has had an effect on usage and content of musical activities in schools for generations, as well as on the formation of musical tastes.

Last, but by no means least, there is the legacy of a clear dichotomy of aims between music education for the masses and music education for the priviledged few, as practised during the eighteenth and nineteenth centuries. This legacy has left confusion over identifying a suitable function for the general music education today which is not to do with learning instruments to play in a band or orchestra or learning to sing so as to be an efficient member of a choir. Central to this confusion is the prevailing attitude towards eighteenth and nineteenth century tonal music involving a generally accepted notion of its exclusive perfection as musical art.

4

TRADITIONAL METHODOLOGIES
Kodaly and Orff

IN Chapter 3 it was seen how music educators in Western culture have been concerned predominantly with developing methods for teaching literacy and vocal skills. Traditionally, this is what is meant by music education. The growth of institutions, first the church, then the state, has helped to establish a music education that is literacy oriented and skill based. While the development of such competencies served some political purpose or social function, they were encouraged by both church and state — one anxious to spread religious teachings, the other to find some ways of civilizing a workforce. Even music education for the privileged involved the acquisition of literacy and motor skills, but here, it was conceded, it was possible to acknowledge the critical role of the listener. In fact during the age of both religious and secular patronage, i.e. the sixteenth to nineteenth centuries, the function of the listener, who was also the employer, became of some importance. At the same time concepts of taste and excellence were being developed. It was soon considered an aristocratic accomplishment to be able to make some kind of critical comment on the quality of a piece of music as well as its execution in performance, and such ideas live on into this century.

The significant point is that this represents another dimension to music education than the mere acquisition of skills and literacy. Clearly, to be able to make such comments with any authority depended upon cognitive abilities rather than those of traditional music education. During the nineteenth century it was noticeable that new types emerged in music: the composer and the commentator on music who were not primarily executants. There were Liszt and Paganini who did not write much of note about music but whose performing was legendary, but there were also Berlioz and Hanslick who could write about music, and in the former case music itself, but whose executant skills were questionable. Thus during the nineteenth century it became established that involvement in music was not confined to composing and performing: the role of the listener and critic was established. It led to some, Debussy for example, turning to writing about music as well as starting a career as a composer.

In these facts lie the seeds of discomfort for music educators today. Does one educate people generally for performing or for listening? Does one develop motor or cognitive musical skills, now that cognitive skills are acceptable in music? To answer both is rather glib and tends to deflate the enormous effort required to gain even a modest accomplishment in performance skills.

Traditional methodologies, that is those which tend to stress motor skills and literacy, live on in this century through the work of two main protagonists: Zoltan Kodaly and Carl Orff. Both base their methods on tradition in the sense that the theoretical background of their educational works conforms more to the type of music education in vogue before the acceptance of the "cognitive musician" referred to.

The Kodaly Choral Method

Kodaly first became interested in school music education during the 1920s. This was prompted by utilitarian needs of a musician: He needed singers to perform his works. In particular he mentions the first performance of *Psalmus Hungaricus* in 1923 in which he had to use boys to strengthen his chorus. So impressed was he by their fine singing that he began an interest that eventually produced his *Choral Method*. Significantly it was during a visit to England in 1927 that he observed the "highly developed singing in schools" there and became aware of the use of hand signals developed by the nineteenth century music educator John Curwen. Kodaly adopted these hand signals for his own method, with some minor modifications. He acknowledges his debt in the foreword to the English edition of his *Choral Method* (1965):

> I am now very pleased to return to the English what I learned from them, and was able to adapt to our needs in Hungary. Because of the warm reception of my previous choruses I hope that my young English-speaking friends will accept the Choral Method in the same way.

The beginnings of the method are described by Lois Choksy (1974 p.7) and show Kodaly's concern over the low standard of musical literacy among student musicians in Hungary. This concern became extended eventually to include the whole population, but it must be emphasized that concern over standards of literacy among music students is one thing, while that over standards among the general populace is another. While the teacher has highly motivated students wishing to improve themselves for professional and vocational reasons the introduction of a method such as Kodaly's can be welcomed by students. Imposing such vocational training on the general populace, however, is quite another matter. Indeed while there is a great deal in Kodaly's work (and other persons' writings on it) concerning the need to develop literacy through vocal ability, even to the extent of advocating that no one should be allowed to play an instrument without first having shown competence as a singer, there is little convincing argument to support the introduction of the method wholesale into schools. Kodaly's notion of making a whole population musically literate appears attractive at first but soon loses this attractiveness as realisation dawns that the method designed for intending musicians needs as much exposure in schools as the teaching of language arts or mathematics for it to be successful in the terms Kodaly would have wished. Indeed the level of success demonstrated by Hungarian children's choirs during the 1960s, which sparked international interest in the method, was brought about by the kind of saturation exposure in Hungarian schools that can be found in the ancient cathedral choir schools of England and Germany, or in special music schools. The method has not demonstrated its effectiveness in the routine of normal schools, and it must be conceded that for it to work as intended the school timetable has to be modified considerably from its present patterns of balanced educational activities for all children.

There is some doubt, therefore, about whom the method is really aimed at. Originally Kodaly was clear in his concern for the level of literacy among music students, and then his concern shifted to the inadequacies of teachers of music in schools. Following this was a further concern over the type of songs used in Hungarian schools. The introduction of folk song in original forms was advocated. The intention was to introduce children to their ethnic roots through music. This was not an uncommon trend in the early years of this century, and evidence of similar ideas can be found all over Europe and North America. In Hungary this was manifest in material for children that comprised folk songs collected by Kodaly and Bartok and introduced during the 1930s and 1940s in Hungarian schools. Initially it was aimed more at the older children than the younger. Later came various texts for younger children, including the *333 Exercises* and notions concerning a "natural song" of children the world over, which became the basis for his compositions for young children. It soon emerged that Kodaly and his associates believed in a natural melodic pattern that occurred in all children. This pattern centres around the interval of a minor third, said to be the easiest interval for children to sing, and includes a falling minor third and an upward perfect fourth, as exemplified in the notes GEAG on the treble stave. Consequently the later developments of the method show this melodic pattern as the starting point for young children in early exposure to pitch concepts of a specific nature.

Whether there is such a thing as a "natural song" sung by children intuitively the world over is pure conjecture and is rather in the same category as other nineteenth century notions such as the belief that there was a "natural" key of the world.

So diverse are the melodic patterns found in music of different cultures that to ascribe common basic configurations is almost the work of a magician. Dr. Ida Halpern (1974) in her extensive investigations into the music of the North American Indian is quite precise in her descriptions of the Indians' use of scales and melody and leaves the reader in no doubt about differences:

In Nootka songs, tonality seems to exist but in no direct relation to any specific existing system . . . to do justice to Indian music, we must revise our western listening habits and our sense of harmony, tonality and rhythm. (pp. 3, 4)

The songs she recorded are full of microtonal intervals and almost unrecognisable intervals larger than a second or a third and generally defying description using the Western system of defining melody. The same can be said of Australian aboriginal music and African tribal music. If such a thing as a "natural melody" were to exist, surely there would be some evidence in aboriginal music? Similarly there is a lack of suitable evidence supporting the notion in early Western music from Gregorian chant onwards. One is tempted to assert that what Kodaly perceived in his investigations into Eastern European folk music was not the basis of the original "natural song" of humanity but merely the cultural habits of that region, which would have some resemblance to Western European music, since it is likely that all of it came out the same Middle Eastern cradle of culture from ancient times. The subsequent cultural effects produced divergence, but some basic similarities remained.

Even ignoring the effects of cultural bias, the different uses of melody worldwide are so diverse that almost the opposite belief to that of Kodaly might be more acceptable. It must be admitted that this is perhaps surprising, since all humans have the same or similar vocal apparatus and bodily configuration, and there are only a limited number of possible pitches of which the human voice is capable. Nevertheless, it is apparent that there is great diversity: There are recorded examples of Tibetan monks who can produce three pitches simultaneously and of North American Indians who can produce two, and the resultant combinations do not resemble anything identifiable in terms of Western harmony. In any case identifying similarities between apparently diverse cultures because of the same or similar origins is not to be confused with the discovery of "natural" behaviour habits to which can be ascribed tendencies common to all members of the human race. In view of our present state of knowledge on these matters it cannot, therefore, be accepted that a "natural song" for children or any other age group applicable to the human race exists. This being the case, Kodaly's and Orff's preference for the falling minor third followed by a rising perfect fourth in their music for children on the basis of its "naturalness" must come into the category of being based on wishfulfillment rather than reliable empirical data. So stereotyped has this melodic pattern become in its association with children (mainly European it must be added) that serious study of it is now probably impossible to conduct, even compensating for the effects of the media and the music educators who have laboured so enthusiastically under such beliefs. As early as the 1920s in England the use of the pentatonic scale was advocated in schools by Walford Davies, and the particular pattern, which is now the basis of Kodaly's method for very young children, was introduced during BBC broadcasts to schools in England at that time.

There is little doubt that the discovery of pentatonic music of the Pacific Rim countries such as Bali, Java, and the whole of Indo-China provided powerful new material for musicians of the late nineteenth and early twentieth centuries. There is evidence, therefore, that the growth of interest in the pentatonic scale emanates from many diverse sources as the science of ethnomusicology emerges. Kodaly's objectives were not confined to those musical, and it is illuminating to examine them and how they might affect applications of the method outside Hungary.

Cecilia Vajda was recommended by Kodaly himself to introduce his method to the students at the Menuhin Music School in London, and she adapted it for use in English schools. In the foreword to Vajda's *The Kodaly Way to Music* (1974) the world-renowned violinist Menuhin states:

> There is certainly no finer form of expression than the communal one of the choral singing and when begun at an early age it enhances the sense of belonging both to a community and to a tradition; it also enhances the well-being — physical, spiritual, and intellectual — of the participants, and it is infinitely valuable in terms both of the individual and of society.

Here Menuhin is reflecting the much older traditional beliefs concerning the function of music, and choral music in particular, in England. The so-called civilizing effects of music have already been referred to earlier, but it is not so much these to which the great virtuoso is referring as to the possibility that the choral tradition in England, so deep rooted for so many centuries, has provided "a counterbalance to all arbitrary forms of composition and music-making which have lost touch with the human condition." It could be deduced from this that Menuhin is hoping that a revival of the choral tradition in schools would halt the progress of much contemporary music that he dislikes as having "lost touch with the human condition." This is not altogether a significant theme in Kodaly's writings or those of his disciples. Menuhin attributes the reason "why British music has evolved so incredibly in the past two decades" to the impetus provided by the choral tradition in England. He appears to refer to what he regards as a traditional culture, but the nature of that culture has already been described. It was not so much traditional and folk-rooted originally as politically and socially expedient in the eyes of either the church or the state. Kodaly had the opposite effect in mind. He saw his choral method as a means of destroying the stultifying effects of choral music imposed by the Germanic church and state in Hungary. He describes how a German song ("Birdie Mine, Singing Fine") was taught by kindergarten teachers as a "Hungarian" song, and it was only after some research himself that he discovered its true origins (Kodaly, 1974). He goes much further than mere criticism of the use of German songs in Hungarian schools:

> Frequently and for a long time I have professed how the soul of the child should be nursed on the mother's milk of the ancient Magyar musical phenomenon; how the Hungarian way of musical thinking could be built and strengthened in it . . . a child nurtured on mixed music will not feel at home anywhere. (p. 153)

Kodaly's theory rests on the belief in nurturing children musically in songs of their own culture, from which they will be able to spread their interests to other cultures. This idea is workable in societies that are not mixed culturally, but today there are very few of this type. Most societies show the effects of massive migrations caused by wars, oppression, famine, etc. In such multicultural situations it is impossible to identify a single culture to which everyone belongs. Kodaly, however, does acknowledge cultural differences: "A great many peoples of the world have their own special tonal system." His case is that in Hungary there was insufficient depth of awareness of the true Hungarian culture: "It is not how a Hungarian performer plays Bach or Beethoven . . . but how he can bring them (the audience) nearer to the Hungarian psyche" (p. 152).

He cites a strong Italian musical identity as an example of what national culture should be. The Italian is recognisable anywhere as

Italian through his music, and "this is already enough to make it clear that something is missing in Hungarian music training" (p. 152).

The adaptation of Kodaly's method to school systems in other countries must rely upon modifying it to suit the cultural traditions of those countries. So special is the Magyar tradition, in Kodaly's own words, that it must mean a great deal of rewriting, since the essence of Kodaly's principles lies in educating young children in their own culture, not an alien one. It also follows that those who might practise the method outside Hungary in its original form are doing what Kodaly criticised in Hungary before the introduction of his method. Impressive though the Hungarian children's choirs are, the philosophical basis of the method and an examination of the culture of each country must present some complicated problems over its educational and cultural appropriateness outside Hungary.

It is clear that the proponents of the Kodaly choral method are aware of the cultural problem. Their solution lies in the belief of a universal "natural" song to be found in all children. This notion plus the suggestion that the method is a "child-developmental" one rather than one based on "subject" is well explicated by Lois Choksy (1974). She explains that the method uses "melodically, the first tones sung by young children (which) are the minor third. They are the tones his mother uses to call him to dinner. They are the tones of many of his own sing-song chants" (p. 16).

If one is objective about this claim then a question has to be asked about the role of the mother. Either the interval of the minor third is a "natural" one, meaning the child will sing it irrespective of his mother's vocal ability as she calls him to dinner, or there is some element of acculturation (he got it from his mother). Does it imply that mothers have a natural song that uses the minor third? If so what about women who are not mothers? Are they not able, or not so prone, to use this interval? At what stage does the proclivity to use a minor third in communications with children first show in mothers? Before giving birth? After?

It must, unfortunately, be concluded that such claims for the naturalness of the minor third, as presented by the Kodaly proponents, appear to be nothing more than myth and fantasy. The same is true of claims concerning the use of rhythm. Choksy explains that "moving rhythms are more child-related than sustained ones. The quarter note is the child's walking pace, the eighth note his running. These are the rhythms of the child's day-to-day living" (p. 16).

There is something fallacious about this. The temporal relationship between quarter notes and eighth notes is mathematically precise; they relate as a ratio of 2:1. Can it be said that children readily understand this precise mathematical relationship through their experience of running being an activity where their legs move or propel them at twice the speed as when walking? Apart from the falsity of the relationship between running and walking as presented in this fashion, it is also false to imagine that people walk rhythmically, either to quarter note patterns or anything else. They don't: Walking is not marching.

Undoubtedly the great strength of the Kodaly choral method lies in its clearly set out sequence of activity and skill acquisition, particularly in the area of music literacy. Historical concepts of good taste also form part of the general ethos, and as the sequence progresses so the student is immersed more and more into a culture that musically is old-fashioned and historically rooted, to say the least, and culturally becomes narrower and more discrete from overall trends in aesthetic experience provided by the performing and expressive arts in today's school curriculum. A more eclectic approach is practised generally in many other subjects in education. Today's classroom is not regarded as a place where a particular culture is deliberately propagated at the expense of providing a broader educational experience in the arts. This is the long-term problem with Kodaly choral method, as Raebeck and Wheeler (1980b) explain:

> Making use of the ideas of Orff and Kodaly is, however, not always easy. Special knowledge and skill are required. Then too, because both men developed their approach to music education in other countries (Orff in Germany and Kodaly in Hungary), their materials and methods are not always relevant to schools in the United States. (p. XV)

They make a further point in advocating that teachers should "read and explore the ideas for experiences suggested, and . . . then adapt them to meet their own classroom situations in the most creative way" (p. XV).

Raebeck and Wheeler also stress that "all activities — speech, melodic, rhythmic and so on — overlap and interweave . . . in the classroom they are best experienced concurrently and in relation with one another" (p. XV).

The point is clearly made that neither the Kodaly nor the Orff method practised alone in its original form can constitute a musical education of sufficient breadth.

With the Kodaly method there is one other reservation: its appropriateness as a vehicle for learning pitch concepts and notations. In the ancient boys' choirs of Europe no such method is now relied upon, yet the standard of musical competence is generally very high. Exposure to music of many different styles and genres and learning about music through living with it in performance is the approach. In this way they are not locked into a narrow stylistic idiom as one is with Kodaly. It is inevitable that with the use of tonic sol-fa, however modified, one is locked into narrow musical style and content. Learning to recognise intervals, with all the literacy that requires, is a much more liberated way of approaching sight singing of pitch, liberated in the sense of being appropriate for all styles and periods of pitch usage. The tonic sol-fa is limiting in that it becomes too cumbersome a language in sight singing vocal music of the twentieth century or earlier than the sixteenth. A facility for reading at sight based upon recognition of intervals is not tied to any single style or period, and this is the method that has evolved in actual practice in choirs in England and elsewhere following the demise of the nineteenth century resurgence of solmisation and the longer established practices of the gamut. In earlier chapters there was reference to the historical traditions of vocal training in the church going back at least as far as the tenth and eleventh centuries. The use of some form of solfège together with various visual aids like the hand or charts with the movable do has been a basic teaching and learning tool in music for the last 800 or 900 hundred years.

In this context Kodaly is yet the latest distinguished proponent of solmisation in a long line of music educators. Throughout the last few hundred years there have been a number of diverse schemes, and each has contributed something by modifying existing practices so as to bring the use of sol-fa up to date with current musical practices. For example, Sarah Glover in late eighteenth century England was one of the first to anglicise the predominantly modal continental system. Kodaly has gone much further than any of his predecessors in structuring and organising the use of sol-fa and visual aids into a coherent system of training and musical education. This achievement is evident and indeed obvious. The problem is not that of effectiveness but rather suitability of aims and content for the end of the twentieth century and the beginning of the twenty-first. Despite the ardour and enormous sincerity of the Kodaly proponents there are unresolved questions concerning the disparity between the musical content of the method and the enormously diverse field of musical practises in this century, and between the educational goals of the method and those considered relevant to an age that is witnessing the growth of electronic technology at a pace that threatens to be overwhelming and whose effects on our lives are already causing serious problems of adjustment. In this context can we find a justification for education in historical idioms and practises, such as those of Kodaly?

There is a further problem: the more pragmatic detail of achieving the goals set by the Kodaly method. It has already been pointed out that more time than is normally allowed music in schools is required for the Kodaly method to operate successfully. Something like a daily lesson is advocated in the early years. If one makes a comparison with the training of choristers in the ancient cathedral choir schools of Europe then some pertinent facts emerge. The purpose of such choir schools is to produce singers who can perform daily in various styles of sacred music in a liturgical context. They are required to sing such a quantity of music that ability to read music is essential for survival, even though quality of sound is perhaps of paramount importance in such choirs. The achievements of choristers in these choirs are perhaps not inimical with those envisaged by Kodaly in his method: in fact he admits as much in his comments on the genesis of his method. To be successful choristers it seems that exposure to music is a significant factor.

A survey carried out by the author (1974) of 22 cathedral and collegiate choirs in England, many with traditions going back almost 1000 years, indicated that an average time for a boy entering a choir at the age of eight years for developing sufficient musical ability to be considered a "useful and efficient member of the choir" was two years, three months. With a daily service and practises, and other musical activities such as learning instruments and practising playing them, there are approximately 20 hours each week of musical involvement for just under 40 weeks each year. This is an exposure to music paralleling that of one's native language in ordinary everyday discourse. It is obvious that a normal school cannot match it in any way and equally obvious that aims to produce such standards are unrealistic in normal schools.

Carl Orff's Music for Children

The emphasis is on rhythmic responses in the *Orff's Music for Children* (Sandvoss, 1976) despite the use of the pentatonic scale in the early stages and the introduction of major and minor scales and basic diatonic harmony in the later ones. The original work, *Musik für Kinder,* was written by Carl Orff and Gunild Keetman (see Orff 1963 and Keetman 1974) and is based on work done in German schools during the 1930s and 1940s. The aims of the Orff method are —

1. to have each child strive for finer discrimination in perception so that everything external to the child's senses is perceived with a greater accuracy and precision;
2. to have the children think about music the way musicians do;
3. to make each child relatively secure and independent rhythmically;
4. to have the children make ensemble music;
5. to have the children improvise creatively (Sandvoss, 1976).

Orff states that "anyone wishing to use his ideas about teaching music to children may advance on his own on the basis of an intimate knowledge of the style of "Musik für Kinder" and grasp of its aims and potential" (Sandvoss, 1976).

The publication that is most often used is that published by Schott in five volumes entitled *Music for Children* with the *Teacher's Manual* by Doreen Hall (1960). This contains the basic ingredients of the method. There are three essential features:

1. the vital importance of movement based on the eurythmics of Emile-Jacques Dalcroze;
2. the use of indigenous folk material as the basic repertoire for speech and song;
3. Orff's historically oriented elemental style found both in the Schulwerk volumes and in his major works (American Orff-Schulwerk Association 1980 Guidelines, p. 1). Activities are based on speech play and the use of simple percussion instruments that are specially designed and require little technique to play. These instruments are based generally on the primi-

tive instruments found in various primitive societies. Thus his method reflects a mixture of influences ranging from the work on eurythmics by the Swiss musician Dalcroze to the predominantly improvised musical activities of South East Asian cultures which tend to use repetition of simple phrases or patterns often superimposed to form a complex tapestry of sound. This is in some ways a forerunner of the minimalist techniques practised by Terry Riley, Steve Reich, and others. Movement, rhythmic vitality, and involvement of the whole body in related movements such as dances or other activities are demanded in the Orff scheme of things. Heightened perception and general awareness together with an enhanced musicality are aimed at. Creative responses in the form of children's own improvisations within the limits set are also encouraged. Questions are often asked though about the role of literacy development, i.e. use of traditional notations and the concentration on physical actions at the expense of more cognitive involvement. At least one piece of research has shown that factors such as enjoyment and popularity rate very highly with the children in Orff-Schulwerk. Margaret Siemens (1969) compared a traditional method with that of Orff and obtained some surprising results. Perhaps the most surprising, in her view, was the higher scores obtained by the control group (traditional) in musical achievement tests of pitch and rhythm. She comments:

If the students have more creative musical activities and many rhythmic exercises one would expect them to become more efficient in identifying pitch and rhythm patterns heard from an instrument. (p. 276).

This need not necessarily occur, and it is likely that a method that stresses pitch and rhythm recognition will yield better scores than one such as Schulwerk. Of more interest and concern are comments such as the following:

Carl Orff's approach to music education for the child begins with the premise that feeling precedes intellectual understanding. (Raebeck & Wheeler, 1980b, p. xix).

In their spontaneous play children become totally involved in rhythmic movement, speech play and chant . . . Carl Orff describes it as "never music alone but forming a unity with movement, dance and speech" . . .

the music making includes singing and playing instruments. (American
Orff-Schulwerk Association 1980 Guidelines, p. 1)

Those who have seen children doing Orff-Schulwerk can be left in
no doubt that there is a high level of commitment and enjoyment apparent. With the right teacher there is a high level of excitement and
involvement, and while it is in no way resembling a visit from a cir-
cus entertainer, these observations of children's responses and attitudes would be applicable to both. The reason for this analogy is to
point out that a high level of excitement, involvement, and commitment is not necessarily related to success in educational activities,
and that the elements that induce such conditions are present in
many types of activities. Many who support Orff-Schulwerk cite the
atmosphere generated as educationally valid evidence. Clearly on its
own it is not.

What then are the educational arguments, besides the excitement
and commitment? The first quotation cited gives a clue. Is the premise correct? Does "feeling" precede intellectual understanding? What
is meant by feeling? The terminology is perhaps ambiguous, but the
intended meaning is clear in the light of all that has been said and
written about Orff's educational philosophy. He believes simply that
children should do things musical rather than sit and learn symbols
for doing things. As Doreen Hall (1960) states,

> in many cases the child is given music lessons as a matter of course, just
> as he receives vitamin pills — Orff has long felt that educationally
> speaking we are putting the cart before the horse; that music is ap-
> proached as an intellectual process which begins with the introduction of
> the staff, the treble clef, middle C and the mathematical division of
> bars. (p. 5)

She goes on to cite the acquisition of language as an example of how
actions precede the use of symbolic representation for them. There is
sound educational reasoning here, as with the following:

> Music educators are becoming increasingly aware of the need for musi-
> cal participation before the child approaches serious study on a chosen
> instrument . . . it seems that the most valuable and musically rewarding
> [method] is one which requires that the child plays an essential role in
> the creation of ensemble music. It is here that we recognize the superior-
> ity of Carl Orff's *Music for Children*. (p. 6)

Musical and Educational Relevance

There is little doubt that a good deal of money spent and time wasted could be avoided if children would learn something about music as suggested before having a violin or flute thrust into their hands. The action involvement of the Orff method is certainly one way, but is it better or worse than the Kodaly method? In some ways they·represent extremes. The former could be said to be motor oriented in that actions rather than exclusively cognitive responses are required, and the latter almost the opposite in that cognitive responses concerning pitch judgements are demanded immediately from children. Yet both methods make similar claims concerning the early training of children, namely that they are child related or justifiable in psychological terms.

Raebeck & Wheeler (1980b) use the word *feeling* and further explicate Orff's premise that ". . . the infant feels the sensations of touch, taste, picking up, throwing etc. . . . long before these are shaped into ideas and verbalized. Once verbalized, considerable time elapses before he learns to read and write about them" (p. xix).

Such arguments have a convincing ring. There can be little doubt that a child feels sensations of the peripheral perceptual systems and the accompanying central processing of information long before he develops the capacity to verbalise about them, let alone write about them and read. The introduction of traditional symbols of musical literacy before the child has experience of what is being symbolised is, as has already been said, "putting the cart before the horse." It is in fact tantamount to teaching verbal language symbols before the child can utter any words. Despite the profession of those propagating Kodaly's method that this crucial sequence of activity and experience precedes abstract symbolisation, there seems precious little time between the experience and activity and the imposition of an abstract symbol. Certainly if an analog is made with language acquisition, then Orff is right. There should be a long period when children merely improvise and grow accustomed to the sounds of music before they begin to use abstract symbolism for those activities.

In the work of Kodaly there appears no musical equivalent in terms of experience to the average 2,000 words that a normal five to six year old has acquired prior to learning the abstract symbols of written language. In this context the method is "putting the cart before the horse!" Unfortunately, in the minds of many persons there is less educational sloppiness in dealing with abstract symbols from the beginning because it can look as though something tangible is being done, and the god of an ill-defined literacy is being placated. Whether there is long-term harm being done to the child's perceptual and intellectual functioning in a musical context is rarely considered. Relevance to the art of music is sometimes difficult to attribute to such educational activities. Common sense, let alone the work of many eminent investigators (Piaget for example), should tell us that the use of abstract symbols before concepts are experienced and understood is pointless. How many adults with no more than grade 8 mathematics could cope with calculus by going straight to the abstract symbols without adequate preparation? In fact, how many adults can go straight to the abstract symbols of music in this way? It could be said that any success of the Kodaly method is due more to a process of osmosis than any definable psychological process of perception and cognition that supports the structure of the method. The importance of regular and frequent exposure would seem to justify this remark.

Another problem with both these methods has already been mentioned, i.e. concerning musical style. The idiom of the musical activities in both is that of an earlier period of musical history, certainly not that of the present. The actual historical period or school of composers is difficult to detect. Neither can it be said that the folk tunes used resemble anything that peasant folk actually sang or played. The use of rhythm and melody is far more subtle in music performed by their originators than one can find in either of these methods. In fact both rhythm and melody have been simplified and made stylistically neutral to enable children to learn the so-called basic musical idioms of Western culture as well as be exposed to their own folk culture. Such a simplification serves neither well: The result is neither folk music nor art music, but a stylistically vague "school music."

Studies of indigenous folk music have demonstrated beyond doubt that the musical idioms used are highly esoteric and relate to no practices in the traditions of Western art music. The use of indigenous music in art music is merely illustration of how it is possible to modify folk music in the interests of art music. Liszt's so-called

"Hungarian" music, and Brahms's, is no more Hungarian than the rest of their output. The simplification of indigenous subtleties to make the music fit Western traditions is not the same thing as contributing to the preservation of folk music, nor is it very useful in introducing children or adults to their "indigneous" culture.

Even within the traditions of Western art music the question of style is of such crucial significance that a simple melodic pattern can assume entirely different meaning in the hands of different composers. For example, a simple scalic passage or an arpeggio motif used as a point of imitation in a Palestrina motet has meaning in terms of the use of imitative counterpoint, Palestrina's fugal procedures, the context of a mode, and the structure imposed by verbal phrases. By contrast the same motif placed as a melodic passage in a Wagner opera has entirely different meaning. Wagner is working to entirely different principles than Palestrina, and he is using different procedures and musical materials in his constructions. Similarly, Handel would give yet another musical significance to this same motif because of his different use of musical materials. The differences between Palestrina, Handel, and Wagner would be not only in the different styles each represents but also in the different musical personalities of the three. Examples are not felt to be necessary, for it is not a difficult task to identify a simple arpeggio in Palestrina and a similar one in Handel or Wagner and examine the different musical meanings the simple arpeggio assumes within the context of each.

If we are to believe the proponents of the methods previously described it would be possible to approach musical art from the neutral ground of a method and move on from such an abstraction to individual styles. This is surely nonsense when the practices of music are considered. It is the same kind of argument that has plagued the musical world since the rise of virtuosity. Can one acquire virtuosity through hard work in technical exercises of the type that emerged in the late eighteenth and nineteenth centuries or through experience with real musical artworks? Musicians have always argued about this during the last 200 years, and the consensus is that little of musical worth can be learned from a diet of technical exercises. Despite the protests from the supporters of Orff and Kodaly, it can only be said that the music contained in their school work for children is little more than a series of technical exercises. In neither method are the crucial issues of musical style and social context addressed.

5

SCIENCE, TECHNOLOGY, AND
MUSICAL PRACTICES

WE are now able to reduce to mathematical formulas the physical nature of the phenomenon called music. As far as the physical properties of sound are concerned, we have the technology to identify all its elements. It should be said, however, that music is more than the sum of its acoustic parts and that this accounts for its mystical nature and artistic function. However, one problem for the music educator is not just whether this is true but how to relate the components of musical sounds with the identifiable components of the physical world. We talk in musical terms of a tune made up of different pitches. In twentieth century science pitch does not exist. Moreover, it is not possible to measure pitch, since it is an entirely subjective judgement on the part of the listener. It is possible to measure the frequency of a pressure wave, which is the nearest science can come to pitch. Similarly, it is not possible to measure loudness. Again this is a subjective judgement, and science can only measure amplitude, which is not necessarily the same thing. The teacher of music is therefore unable to explain precisely and scientifically what it means to be in tune or to get louder. The human voice is capable of using different tuning systems to that of say the piano, and the violin is capable of a much more flexible tuning than say the trumpet. The reasons are partly the physical nature of each, partly the ability of the performer to make an appropriate (or inappropriate) mental adjustment and action. In harmony there is no scientific basis for dissonance; again it is entirely a subjective matter dependent upon the individual's training, preference, and the style referred to. The music educator is, therefore, unable to use modern technological knowledge in his teaching of concepts such as pitch, dynamics, harmony, and even rhythm. A brief examination of the details will expose the nature of the difficulties. There are two aspects: one is acoustics, which is physical events that stimulate the sensory mechanisms of hearing, and the other is psychoacoustics, which is the study of responses to auditory sensations. One is a study of the physical properties of auditory events, whereas the other concerns human psychological behaviour in response to events.

Hearing and Interpreting Sound

When we hear music we are making subjective judgements concerning what we call pitch, timbre, rhythm (including phrase or sentence length), and loudness. In reality we are hearing the acoustic phenomena of frequency, duration, and amplitude, and the various interactions of these elements. Frequency is the term given to the number of times a cycle of vibration occurs in a given amount of time, usually a second, and precise tunings have long been the subject of disagreement. For example, in 1939 it was agreed internationally that the frequency to be used for concert A (2nd space in the treble stave) should be 440 cycles per second. Until this agreement it had varied from nineteenth century standards of 450 cps at Covent Garden, London, to 461.6 cps in North America, or even 435 cps in France. (Jeans 1961, p. 24). Thus the pitch of concert A is not a naturally occurring phenomenon but an agreed standard frequency that is used as a reference point for pitch. Most sounds comprise a combination of frequencies rather than a single pure tone. A descant recorder, for example, or a clarinet, is capable of producing a single frequency with little distortion caused by additional frequencies (or partials). On an oscilloscope this event would look like a series of half circles, one above an imaginary middle line followed by one below, and repeated. As partials (or other frequencies) are added, the relative purity of the circle shape becomes distorted, producing a more complex wave form. Complexity of wave form is one element in judgements concerning timbre, but it is also an element in pitch judgements since complex forms can tend to emphasise the fundamental tone for the listener.

The distance between the highest point of the wave and the following lowest point is called the amplitude. The greater this distance (or the larger the wave shape) the greater is the disturbance, or pressure, caused by the wave. We hear these differences as variants of loudness, but there are other factors than mere amplitude that affect our judgement of relative loudness. Very low sounds always tend to sound quieter than higher ones, for example, often irrespective of amplitude because of the nature of our auditory apparatus.

Duration of a sound is relatively simple to define. It relates to the length of time, in whatever unit of measurement is being used, that a sound is perceived to have lasted before it is either repeated or is replaced by another sound. From this we perceive elements of rhythm, but again, rhythm is not solely a function of duration of sounds. Elements of loudness, perceived as accents, can have rhythmic meaning for us.

Thus relationships between the acoustic and psychoacoustic events are not at all simple or straightforward. It cannot be said that, psychologically, pitch varies simply as a function of frequency, or that timbre varies as a function of combined frequencies, or that loudness varies solely as a function of amplitude. There is a relationship between the pairs listed, but it is complex and is subject to interference from other aspects. For example, Radocy and Boyle (1979) cite the "classic study of Stevens (1935) . . . as evidence that the pitch of a tone can change with an increase in the intensity of a tone sounding with constant frequency" (p. 15).

Davies (1978) illustrates diagrammatically the effects of amplitude variations upon pitch perception:

> Put very simply, tones of high pitch appear to go higher as they become louder, and low tones appear to become lower. There is a range in the middle of the audible frequency band where there is little effect upon pitch as a result of intensity change. (p. 43)

He explains further that other experiments have shown that the same thing happens if it is tried the other way around, when intensity is held constant for a tone of 1000 Hz, and subjects are asked to match another in terms of loudness, by changing the frequency. Again, tones of different pitches are set at different intensities in order to make them sound equally loud. This confirms the nature of the interaction between pitch and loudness. (p. 43)

On the same topic Winckel (1967) states, "Through some simple experiments it can be shown that there is no absolute measure for pitch and dynamics for the ear" (p. 91).

He explains further that "frequent dynamic changes in low and very high notes in a piece of music . . . lead to noticeable distuning, while this will be very small in the middle frequency area" (p. 93). There are many complicated aspects of the effects of frequency and amplitude on the perceptual mechanism. Some can be explained physiologically as a function of the mechanical movements of the basilar membrane and the resultant input to the parts of the brain dealing with auditory sensations. Clearly in this case the factor of innate physical endowment is present: Some people will have basilar membranes that respond more appropriately than others. Other explanations are psychological and are a function of the perceptual processes of the individual. Here experience and training are important factors.

Winckel (1967) examines the effectiveness of the ear in responding to intensity or amplitude of acoustic events. He states that "just as in the case of frequency, intensity of sound events is not evaluated uniformly. The limitation exists that the ear does not respond equally to all frequencies" (p. 97). He goes on to explain some of the details:

The ear has a particularly high sensitivity between 2000 and 3000 cps. At lower frequencies the sensitivity of the ear is reduced as the loudness decreases. For a tone of 40 phons (loudness approximately "piano" in musical terms) for example, one must use at 120 cps ten times the sound pressure as for a tone of 1000 cps. (p. 99)

Pitch perception is also affected by the type of wave formation. Radocy and Boyle (1979) explain that "a complex tone with component frequencies of 100, 200, 300, 400 and 500 Hz will make a wave with a repetition frequency of 100 Hz" (p. 20). This will be the perceived pitch because of the "process of fundamental tracking, which yields a sensation of periodicity pitch" (p. 21). Periodicity, or the repeat of the wave form, is the factor that enables us to assign pitch.

What Does It Mean To Be In Tune?

It follows from the above simplified evidence that there is no such thing as natural laws of pitch, dynamics, or timbres as they occur in music. They are in fact inventions of man's psychological processes, and as such they have to be learned; one is not born with the ability to discriminate differences in any, merely the ability to discriminate alterations in the stimulation of the sensory organs. The same applies to tuning systems. The earliest modern tuning system is the Pythagorean scale, which was devised by Pythagoras about 550 BC and was in use until the fifteenth century. He "assigned to his C exactly $1^1/_2$ times the frequency of F, to his G exactly $1^1/_2$ times the frequency of C and so on, thus arriving at a scale . . ." (Jeans, 1961, p. 167).

The intervals between the notes a whole tone apart in this scale were exactly equal, that is with a frequency ratio of 9:8 each. One of the problems arises with what we call the semitone. Pythagoras called it a hemitone, and it is less than halfway between those notes a tone apart, and therefore smaller than the modern semitone. Such a system was inadequate for instruments that were capable of chromaticism, since enharmonic tones are not equivalent and it was, therefore, impossible to modulate within this system of tuning in the modern styles.

Another system led to the scale known as the mean tone scale. In this system the ratios of certain intervals were altered for aesthetic reasons. For example, the frequency ratio between E and C is 5.06 on the Pythagorean scale, whereas one of 5.0 is more pleasurable to the ear. To obtain 5.0 meant altering the ratios of the intervals between C and G, and others a fifth apart, to 1.495 instead of 1.5. This gave the desired ratio between E and C but had the effect of distorting the ratios between some other notes. It meant that musicians had to avoid writing or playing in certain keys.

The solution that enabled musicians to play and compose music in any key was a tuning system called *equal temperament*. In this system all semitones were equal and represented the same frequency ratio, 1.05946. This had been calculated by the French mathematician Mersenne in 1636, but it was much later in the seventeenth century that the system began to be employed.

Another system of tuning called *just intonation* appeared during the fifteenth and sixteenth centuries and attempted to establish itself using simple ratios between tones. The problem with this was that it was not suitable for later Western tonal music since it had no uniform fifth between all notes a fifth apart, and again, modulation was not possible.

Radocy and Boyle (1979) cite Nickerson in explaining the complexities of tuning and intonation during musical performance nowadays. They describe how he

> analyzed performances of string quartets, both in isolation, and ensemble. From his analysis he concluded that 1) performances do not conform completely to just, Pythagorean, or equal temperament, 2) performances of melodies both solo and ensemble approach Pythagorean tuning. (p. 133)

They conclude that "there is need for much research on the matter of intonation" after indicating that "good intonation is not any one basic tuning system used exclusively" (p. 133).

Davies (1978) provides further examples of problems associated with tuning. He states that

> even on fixed pitch instruments, like the piano, where the performer has no control over the state of tuning of the instrument during a performance, there is no unanimity about the frequencies to which it is tuned . . . . a piano tuner . . . tunes it until it sounds right to him, not until it is right. (p. 54)

He cites examples of distuning functions in clarinets, trumpets, and pianos, all caused by physical conditions found in the instrument. Furthermore, it is the job of the performer, in the case of the wind instruments, and the tuner, in the case of the piano, to compensate for these deficiencies. The problems of scales, tuning of instruments, and intonation have troubled musicians for centuries, long before there were any reliable scientific methods of measuring ratios and tensions of strings, not to mention thickness and shape of wood or metal piping and consistency of reverberating material. Nowadays the situation is different. Reliable scientific methods and equipment exist. The problem lies in the difficulties of matching up the musician's intuitive approach to such problems with scientific enquiry and data, or with a particular musician's or group of musicians' personal tastes in such things. Some choirmasters will, for example, alter the pitch of major and minor thirds in the quest for the right (to them) tuning of a chord. This can cause problems for the performer playing an accompanying instrument with monochrome tuning, such as the piano.

Performers may well be mixing up several systems of tuning in the process of searching for the right sound. The process, however, owes nothing to science; it is entirely intuitive. The question to be asked is whether there is such a state as perfect tuning, applying to all instruments, and to human voices, simultaneously, for use with tonal or modal music. Some systems are more suitable for tonal works, and others are more suitable for modal music. Radocy and Boyle (1979), quoting Barbour, explain that just intonation might be satisfactory in modal music such as that of Palestrina. Clearly, such tuning would not be at all pleasing in tonal music, since it was the introduction of equal tuning of all semitones that made tonal music possible in the music of the eighteenth and nineteenth centuries.

Since neither researchers nor musicians can agree on universals for tuning systems, the music educator in schools has few or no agreed musical or scientific principles upon which to base pitch training in young children. For example, in the first stages of Kodaly training where the interval of a minor third is important, what precise minor third is the teacher to use as she asks the children to imitate her? After all, children have acute auditory sensitivity and will imitate exactly the tuning they are presented with. Are they to be presented with mean, just, Pythagorean or equal tuning?

A good deal of effort has been spent on explaining the problems of tuning, since it is felt by many researchers that the ability to pitch accurately is the most important ability in musical behavior. This ability is manifest in two ways; one in recognition tasks, where the subject is asked to identify intervals, or distunings, and the other in behavioural tasks where the subject is asked to reproduce a particular interval or pitch. Such tasks form the basis of Kodaly training and other methods of voice training. If children, or anyone, are asked to learn something, then it should be capable of precise definition in terms of its identifiable properties, and the problems of learning pitch become compounded if pitch is not seen as something relating to musical style rather than some neutral absolute. It has been shown that tuning systems are many and varied and tend to serve the type of music they are best suited for, but even then performance practices vary so greatly that there is a mixture of different systems in all performances. Clearly we are talking about an art, not something capable of reduction to mechanical rules.

Learning pitches involves learning artworks using scale systems, or one single scale system. Again the problem is similar to that relating to tuning systems; indeed the two are closely connected. Mursell (Radocy & Boyle, 1979) explains that a scale in music has a twofold significance: (1) It is a social phenomenon and (2) It facilitates tonal relationships (p. 107). He explains further that scales are not a manifestation of some mathematical ideal; they are not capable of rationalization in terms of mathematical ratios or logic. Moreover, there is no such thing as a "natural" scale. He states categorically that "there is nothing in the entire theory of music upon which more perverse quasi-mathematical ingenuity has been wasted than the scale" (p. 108).

All scale systems, and indeed all musical phenomena, are entirely the inventions of man, and music is a sociocultural phenomenon. This being the case, the teacher of music who expects children to learn tonal music is required to work out very carefully which systems of tuning are to be used and to take into account that the process involves learning precise behavioural responses that are not innate, natural, or capable of manifestation except in imitation, either of the teacher or of others in the circle of acquaintances of the pupil.

How Natural is Rhythm?

Rhythmic behavior is subject to the same conditions. Rhythm is also an invention of man and is not a manifestation of some natural law. It can be said that rhythm is an indispensible element in music, since durational values of some kind have to occur in music, but various theories of the origins of rhythm have no scientific basis. The great music educator Emile-Jaques Dalcroze (1967) believed strongly in the theory that the "natural" rhythms of the body provide the origins of the rhythms of music. He wrote:

> . . . a child's body possesses instinctively the essential element of rhythm which is sense of time. Thus: 1) The beats of the heart, by their regularity, convey a clear idea of time, but they are a matter of unconscious activity, independent of the will, and therefore valueless for the purposes

of execution and perception of rhythm. 2) The action of breathing provides a regular division of time, and is thus a model of measure. The re-
spiratory muscles being subject to the will, in however qualified a
degree, we are able to operate them rhythmically, that is to say, to divide
the time and accentuate each division by a stronger muscular tension. 3)
Regular gait furnishes us with a perfect model of measure and the division of time. (p. 38)

The basis of his method of musical training, called *eurythmics*,
was, therefore, the natural rhythms of the body: the heartbeat,
breathing, and walking. He stressed the vital importance of rhythm
to all music and saw it as the first and primary training of a musician. However, there is little evidence to support the notion that the
natural rhythms of the body have much to do with the rhythms of
music, as they are manifest in responses to musical rhythms. Radocy and Boyle (1979) quote a number of researchers who have explored the origins of rhythm, including Mursell, who "criticizes the
heart beat notion on the basis that there is no mechanism known to
physiology by which the heart beat gives us our sense of timing" (p.
77). The same authors cite Lund: "The theory that the preferred
'true beat' in music is conditioned by some regularly recurrent physiological process has no support from the data of this study" (p. 78).
They again quote Mursell:

> Mursell notes that attempts to explain rhythm in terms of regularly recur-
> ring bodily processes overemphasize the regularity of rhythmic occur-
> rence. By and large attempts to support physiological theories have relied
> upon correlations, real or otherwise, between tempi of music of selected
> composers and the various rates of physiological process. (p. 78)

Radocy and Boyle go on to dismiss such connections because of
extreme variability of the so-called rhythms of the human body and
their complexity as a means of explaining rhythmic responses to "relatively short-term musical stimuli." Lund explains as follows:

> Responsiveness to rhythm is learned and cannot be accounted for solely
> by any . . . theories (of natural body rhythms). Response to rhythm in-
> volves the total organism and cannot be explained in either/or terms of
> musical or mental activity. (p. 106)

Rhythmic behaviour is, therefore, a learned response involving
the auditory perceptual mechanisms as well as motor activities. This
view is held by many researchers in the field. The music educator is

again faced with training where rhythm is concerned rather than trying to elicit some natural response from the child. The choices facing him/her are related to style, type of rhythm, and context, not to the body's natural rhythms and matching these to some musical stimuli.

Early Renaissance Science and Music

During the twelfth and thirteenth centuries, scholars were beginning to rediscover Greek scientific thought. There is evidence of a growing awareness of an empiricist approach to the phenomena of music as opposed to the older notions of the "divinity" or "naturalness" of musical sounds. Lang (1941) states that

> Odington (d.c. 1330) doubts outright the empirical-sonorous existence of musica mundana (a notion attributed to Boethius) and his scientific treatment shows a thoroughly practical, modern conception of the nature of music. (p. 139)

Secular notions about anything in medieval times were opposed in some religious quarters. Music was regarded as particularly sacred, and secular theories that music could be manipulated in a "scientific," i.e. mathematical, manner ran contrary to older ideas of the God-centred order of things. However, by the fourteenth century the march of scientific thought had produced some effects in music. Philipe de Vitry (1291-1361), a learned bishop and musician, produced a theoretical tract entitled "Ars Nova." In it were quite revolutionary notions of a mathematical nature concerning musical rhythms and their notations. One of the most influential was that concerning binary rhythm. This was considered to be a "tempus imperfectum," as opposed to the theologically sanctified "tempus perfectum" — triple time. De Vitry's role is described by Lang (1941) as one that clarifies existing practices, and his achievement was

> to sanction and expound the musical innovations of the Ars Nova which he did with remarkabled lucidity . . . by the addition of coloured red notes permitting graphic indication of complicated rhythms, triplets, syncopation, etc. (p. 149)

This was a big blow to the theologians who clung to older ideas that did not allow for such an intrusion of man's manipulative powers. Music was to be seen in a different light, as a kind of scientific activity that was subject to mathematical laws of construction. This development, along with others, made possible the work of the great Renaissance masters of the 16th century.

New Technology and Its Effects on Music

The impact of technological development also had its effects on music and musical concepts. In the seventeenth century, for example, French makers of the transverse flute introduced a conical rather than the usual cylindrical bore. This produced a smoother tone and made the instrument more suitable for mixing with strings and other instruments. With a straight bore the sound tended to be more shrill, suitable only for military bands. To make this possible there had to be suitable tools capable of boring in such a fashion, and craftsmen with the skill. The technological advances of the sixteenth and seventeenth centuries made it possible. The point is that the orchestra, as we now see it, includes the flute by accident, not design. There would have been no orchestral flute had not this alteration in its capabilities been developed through advancing technology.

The same is true of many instruments during the period 1600 to 1800. Many underwent fundamental changes in their capabilities because of technological innovation in their construction. Obviously there were social and musical pressures for such changes, but there had to be an adequate technology to bring them about. Another example of the effect of technology on musical instruments, and therefore on musical practices, can be seen in the development of the piano. During the eighteenth century the enormous tension of all the strings combined was held by a wooden frame, and this was not always reliable, either in holding tensions steady for stable tuning or in standing up to combined tensions without collapsing. Apart from the invention of the check-action, late in the eighteenth century, which enabled the string to vibrate freely because of a simple mechanism that threw the hammer back off the string once it had hit it, the most important innovation was the introduction of the iron frame. This was capable of withstanding much greater tensions than wood; strings could be longer and stronger, and therefore the piano became a much more powerfully expressive instrument. In turn the music of Chopin, Schumann, Liszt, Rachmaninov, and others who explored a great expressive sonority of which the piano was now capable, was possible. Without the developments referred to, these composers could not have produced the music they did.

In the present century many technical innovations have shown up in musical practices, most obviously the use of a great variety of electronic devices for generation, amplication, and manipulation of sound. The possibility of generating sound electronically resulted in the development of electronic organs during the 1930s and 1940s. By means of oscillators, synthesized tones could be produced and combined to form any combination of which the instrument was capable. Thus one could synthetically produce the sound of a trumpet, for example, or any instrument, provided the correct number and intensity of partials was known and reproduced. It was not until the 1950s, when recording techniques developed the use of the tape, that electronic music in a compositional sense was possible. Once the tape became a tool available to the composer, any sound was available for use in composition. Moreover, any rapid change from one type of sound to another also became possible.

This meant that a composer had at his disposal a greater range of sound than ever before. For example, in conventional music, using conventional instruments that is, approximately seven octaves or 84 different pitches are available. Using electronic instruments, thousands of pitches are available, but they cease to be pitches in electronic music in the traditional sense. They are frequencies. Clearly the listening public has to adapt to new parameters of high and low sounds, but this is no different from the changes in rhythmic acceptance required for the music of the "Ars Nova," except in degree. Similarly, there are about seven different levels of dynamics possible in conventional music. They range from *fff* down to *ppp*, though there is doubt among some that even this range is possible on conventional instruments. With electronic instruments hundreds of different levels of amplitude are possible. In pitch movements from one level to another, the speed with which a performer can execute such a change is a function of the capabilities of the instrument and her/his technique. With electronic instruments a glissando of, say, from 18,000 cps to 10 cps is possible in the shortest time the composer requires. Again the question of whether we can hear all these events is important, but the ear and the auditory apparatus can now cope with the complexities of a modern orchestra, which would undoubtedly have terrified medieval man. We obviously have great capacity to adapt.

With duration, any kind of subdivision of time units can be prepared. Clearly, the units would be measured in seconds or related units rather than the notional units of half or quarter notes, etc., used in conventional music. Since this kind of technology is available, it is unthinkable that composers should ignore it. They have never shown a proclivity to ignore new ideas and materials in the past, and show no inclination to do so in the present.

The use of electronic devices in music is now very widespread and ranges from deliberate manipulation of sounds for effect, to compositional works of a serious nature, to electronic means of producing high quality recordings from symphony orchestras or other artists, whereby the short extract can be built up into a complete piece by adding others through the use of splicing techniques to produce the error-free performance.

Some Psychoacoustic Consideration

Scientific developments of this century have led, inevitably, to scientific investigation into human behaviour. In the past this was of a speculative, philosophical nature; nowadays it is of a more empirical kind whereby controlled conditions are used to observe the effects of some variable on behaviour. In such experiments we are not able to examine the effects of music so much as the effects of tiny manipulations of some aspects of sound. Thus it is possible to examine auditory responses to, say, tiny movements in the frequency or amplitude of a sound. For the music educator this can be of some value. If, for example, he/she wishes to teach the movement of a whole tone up and down, i.e from C to D, it is necessary to know that children are capable of discriminating such differences along this parameter. More important, it is useful to know what the smallest movement is that children can perceive.

It has already been stated that pitch varies partly, but not exclusively, as a function of frequency variation. However, each variation in frequency does not necessarily produce a sensation of change of pitch in the listener, other variables being controlled. There is a concept of just noticeable difference (jnd), which is the amount the frequency must be changed in order for a listener to detect a difference. Unfortunately there are no simple rules for describing such an event. The size of the jnd varies according to a number of factors. It has already been pointed out that changes in amplitude can give a listener the effect of a change in pitch even though the frequency remains constant. There is also a variation in jnd that is dependent upon the frequency. It is smaller at lower frequencies and larger at higher ones. Another contributing factor is length of time the listener is exposed to the sound. There is a vital connection between length of time and periodicity as far as the human ear is concerned. If the sound does not last long enough there will be no effect of periodicity for the listener and therefore no sensation of pitch.

The distance and position of the listener in relation to the source of the sound are other factors contributing to jnd size. Sergeant (1973) explains that

> if a test is given in a classroom, children seated at a distance from the sound source, or in a portion of the room subject to acoustic dampening will hear the tones at a lower sensation level than children more favourable sited. Much larger difference-limens (or jnds) will be apparent to those disadvantaged by their classroom location, and these children will in effect receive a more difficult test. (p. 7)

He goes on to describe an experiment that demonstrates loss of intensity in different areas of a room when a pure-tone signal was sounded. The range of variation, taking the room as a whole, was from 0 db to in excess of 25 db. Clearly this factor can have an important effect on students in a classroom.

In general terms psychological investigation has demonstrated that the factors affecting a response are extremely complex and are functions variously of the stimulus itself, the person affected by the stimulus, and the conditions under which the stimulus and the person meet. Miller (1964) states that

> more and more psychologists who study perception . . . are beginning to ask how can I discover the transformations that a perceiver can impose upon the information he takes in? And with each step forward in understanding the transformations, one gains increased respect for both the complexity and the beauty of our perceptual machinery. (p. 113)

So far we have examined some aspects of musical sound, namely its acoustic properties, and how the listener tends to be influenced by one or more aspects. Most important, however, it has been explained how complex is the perceived relationship between the various physical properties of the phenomenon we call sound. The reasons for this emanate from two things: one the physical limitations of man's peripheral perceptual apparatus (in this case the ear), the other the nature of man's psychological behaviour.

Many writers explain how the basilar membrane mechanically excites the nerve endings so that signals are passed to the brain for central processing. The excitement of the membrane is caused by pressure waves, which we call sound. Experiments have shown that the membrane has limitations in its ability to respond to sound and that certain parts of it are more receptive to certain characteristics of sound than others. Furthermore, this tends to vary with each individual. For example, the experiments of Stevens, Davis, and Lurie (Radocy & Boyle, 1979) show that higher tones tend to stimulate the membrane near the oval window, tones around 2000 Hz near the middle, and lower tones near the far end. This experiment was carried out using guinea pigs, whose cochleas closely resemble those of humans. In the case of humans the stimulation areas have been mapped by Von Bekesy (Radocy & Boyle, 1979). These show that 5000 Hz stimulate the membrane about 10 mm from the base at the oval window end, and the relatively low frequency of 200 Hz has its resonance maximally about 300 mm from the base (apex end). This indicates that there is a physiological basis for the internal act of perception; more important, since each person will have slight differences in physiological makeup, there will be corresponding differences in perception. It is important to realize, however, that perception is regarded as a unified process involving the complete organism so that when we hear, our perception of what we hear is likely to be affected by what we see, or feel, or even taste, as well as what we have experienced previously in any or all of these modalities. Concerning this particular point, Bruner (1973) says,

> For as L.L. Thurstone has put it "in these days when we insist so frequently on the interdependence of all aspects of personality, it would be difficult to maintain that any of these functions, such as perception, is isolated from the rest of the dynamical system that constitutes a person." The problem is, indeed, to understand how the process of perception is affected by other concurrent mental functions and how these functions, in their turn, are affected by the operation of the perceptual processes. (p. 44)

While we may be able to present information of an atomized nature with some precision, that is concerning discrete aspects of sound or parts of the sounds we call music, we cannot supply much information about the total process of perception of such sounds or about the total sound itself as an object of perception. While we can be certain that under some circumstances it will prove difficult for us to hear certain pitches as we want them heard (because of amplitude variations or placement in a room for example), we cannot ignore the whole person and the wealth of experience that may lie behind the act of perception. We can say that someone with little or no experience of a particular tonal interval, say a perfect 5th, might be disadvantaged if placed in a "bad" spot of a room, as suggested by Sergeant (1973). Someone with a great deal of experience, placed in the same spot, would be able to compensate for the deficiences of the sound by virtue of experience. He/she would make a mental adjustment and supply the missing information or alter the distorted signal so that it conformed to what experience dictates it should be. In the same way our perceptual apparatus tends to interpret rather than merely absorb information, and interpretation means supplying additional information to make something fit our experience. Bryant (1974) explains that "past experience is . . . crucially important . . . it must influence the way a person perceives" (p. 4).

For the music educator this means that there can be little reliance upon a notion of objective information content of musical sounds. Apart from the problems of defining their physical characteristics in relation to the practises of music, there is an additional complication possible in the experience or lack of it on the part of the listener and the proclivity to hear what we want to. Bruner (1973) explains the problem:

> The organism exists in a world of more or less ambiguously organised sensory stimulation. What the organism sees, what is actually there perceptually represents some sort of compromise between what is presented by the autochthonous processes and what is selected by behavioural ones . . . such selection, we know, is determined not only by learning . . . but also by motivational factors. (p. 46)

We cannot even rely on the pupil, for example, actually taking notice of his perceptual apparatus. He may well have perceived an alteration in pitch caused by amplitude variation but responds to the amplitude difference rather than the illusion of pitch change. Or, thinking that the teacher wants a particular answer, he might deny the facts as presented by his sensory input and supply what he feels is desired, namely a response indicating pitch change. Factors such as intelligence, honesty, and general personality traits also come into the picture. The ability of the mind to override sensory input is well documented, e.g. Gregory (1960).

Music of today tends to reflect theories of perception and cognition, much as music of the past reflected philosophical notions already referred to. Modern theories of perception of sound are reliant upon knowledge about the nature of sound. The ability now available to identify elements of sound referred to here has naturally had some impact upon the work of composers and performing musicians. Something of the nature of this impact is explained in the next chapter.

6

THE 20th CENTURY
A Communication Explosion in Music

Multicultural Influences in Music

BEETHOVEN was in the habit of arranging for first performances of his symphonies in as many as three or four major
European cities simultaneously and not just to outwit the musical
"crooks" who took advantage of the lack of copyright laws. Yet even
he could not have wished for greater exposure than that which occurred for the slow movement of his third Symphony at the Munich
Olympics, following the murder of the young Jewish athletes. Many
millions of people in the world shared the experience of hearing the
music from the Olympic stadium by means of satellite transmission
across the planet. In Beethoven's day news of any sort had to be
transmitted through carriers on horseback, and this took a long
time. The impact of news events was correspondingly less immediate and sensational. Today there is a "new" sensation every day. The
broadcasting media ensure this by searching the globe for suitable
events. Thus we are not surprised to hear about southern Africa, Japan, the Antarctic, and Alaska all in the same news bulletin. Consequently, we are becoming familiar with different peoples, different

life-styles, different attitudes, and of course, different cultural habits. We are no longer surprised to have contact with languages and music of different lands and take it as a matter of course that information of this type is available for daily consumption on television, in the newspapers, or on the radio.

Consider the variety of different cultural stimulation available today compared with that during Beethoven's lifetime. For Beethoven the life-styles and cultural confines of Vienna formed the boundaries of his experience. He had no access to information from all corners of the globe, or even from many areas of the rest of Europe. Some of his music related as far as it was possible to events that he knew about in the world, but his world was a small one, almost exclusively confined to Western Europe. It is pointless to speculate what he might have produced had he experienced the kind of exposure to the world's cultures that is possible today, but it is difficult to imagine an artist of any description being unmoved at all by the information explosion referred to. Today the evidence is that artists do respond readily to this environment, even though they do not respond uniformly. The response is not just a superficial incorporation of new, exotic sounds; it reflects a much deeper process involving philosophical concepts of life, death, and the growing awareness of the diversity of life on the planet. This is evident in the work of many artists, and discussion of the work of a few composers will suffice to illustrate.

Benjamin Britten, for all his English reserve and sensitivity, was not just deeply moved by his experiences of Japanese Noh plays, his artistic output was influenced. He visited Japan in 1956 and was so impressed, particularly by the *Sumidagawa* of Juro Motomasa (1395-1431) that he incorporated certain constructional principles into "Curlew River," first performed at the 1964 Aldeburgh Festival (*see* Evans, 1979). Not only did the whole concept of the Noh play fascinate him, but Japanese music also had its impact, so much so that Peter Evans was moved to write,

> Curlew River was the least predictable work the composer had written
> for many years, and it retains, even when very familiar, its power to en-
> close the listener in a unique world of feeling. (p. 469)

Evans is referring, undoubtedly, to the use of Japanese-inspired sounds and the flavour the whole work has as a result.

Another example shows a Russian, formed intellectually in Paris, who upon coming into contact with the vibrant and virile popular music from North America found his sensibilities so affected that he incorporated some popular rhythms into his compositions. For example, in 1920 the first performance of "Ragtime" took place in London. The idea of the work was to

> produce a composite portrait of the new type of popular dance music that had just emerged from North America giving it the importance of a concert piece, as in the past composers had done for the minuet, waltz, mazurka and so on. (White, p. 276)

In these examples Stravinsky was employing the time-honoured device of transmuting sounds from popular music into serious artwork. Composers who have done this are legion: The Renaissance polyphonists in their masses and the symphonists in their sonata structures are two great categories where this has occurred extensively, and Stravinsky makes the point that he is doing no more than they did in the use of the minuet in the eighteenth century.

Karlheinz Stockhausen (born 1929) composed a piece of what he described as "world communication music." Its title, *Telemusik*, implies music for communication, and it was realised in tape form in the Electronic Studio of Japanese Radio in Tokyo in 1966. In the work he uses folk music from many parts of the world and fuses or synthesizes it electronically into a unified musical statement. The composer explains, "In all this I wanted to come closer to an old dream — going one definite step further in the direction of writing not 'my' music, but a music of the whole world" (Wörner, 1973 p. 58). He uses music from places as diverse as Hungary, Bali, Spain, Vietnam, and South America. The thirty-two sections or structures of the piece are defined by various Japanese percussion instruments, and each section is an auditory experience wholly relevant to this age of electronics.

John Cage (born 1912) has been a major influence in some aspects of twentieth century art. He has rejected Western ideas of art music and taken instead Eastern influences and models as his guide. His interest in and practising of Zen Buddhism has been one major influence, resulting in the concept of indeterminacy, whereby either the performer is encouraged to participate more in determining the events of a composition or the random happenings of certain locations have this function. An example of this kind of composition is "Solo for Voice no. 2," where the singer prepares a programme of agreed length using various combinations of her own choosing from six transparent sheets containing various shapes for interpretation in sound. His "Music of Changes" for piano uses number sequences found in the *I Ching* as a basis for musical actions. Other works show the influence of the Javenese gamelan orchestra, including "Sonatas and Interludes" for prepared piano. In this a piano has various muting devices such as rubber tubing, stove bolts, and weather stripping inserted between the strings at certain points so as to simulate the percussion sounds of the gamelan orchestra. He wrote works that are more determinate, but these also display non-European influences. An example is "First Construction in Metal," a work for various percussion instruments, including brakedrums and metal sheets. In 1937, Cage explained his position in a talk he gave in Seattle:

> If this word music is sacred and reserved for 18th century and 19th century instruments, we can substitute a more meaningful term; organized sound . . . percussion music is a transition from keyboard influenced music to the all-sound music of the future. (Cage, 1968, p. 5)

Cage, despite his musical training in North America, which included two years of study with Schoenberg between 1935 and 1937, is very much a product of twentieth century influences formed by increased communications and breaking down of cultural barriers. Clearly the very traditional training in Western harmony that he received from Schoenberg had little of its intended effect on him. Yet another example will help illustrate how composers of this century cannot but be influenced by it. Iannis Xenakis, born in Greece in 1922, became directly involved in anti-Nazi resistance, and the influence on the growing artistic sensitivity of the adolescent became profound.

> In my music there is all the agony of my youth, of the Resistance, and the aesthetic problems they posed, with the street demonstrations, or even the occasional, mysterious deathly sounds of those cold nights in December 1944 in Athens. From this was born my conception of the massing of sound events, and therefore of stochastic music. (Whittall, 1977, p. 239)

Xenakis believes that mathematics has a vital role to play in the evolution of modern music. He sees mathematics as a "working tool" in composition. As Whittall comments, "on this basis, the desire to create a completely new world on the ruins of the old rather than from those ruins, becomes understandable" (Whittall, 1977, p. 239). Xenakis explains further that stochastic laws "are laws of the passage from complete order to total disorder in a continuous or an explosive manner" (Whittall, 1977, p. 240). Two such works are "ST/4-1,080262" and "ST/10-1,080262," both completed in 1962. The title of each is explained by Whittall (1977): "The first piece of stochastic music for four and ten instruments respectively, using calculations made by computer on the 8th February 1962" (p. 240). Conventional instruments are used: for example, in "ST/4," a string quartet and conventional notations are employed to help translate the computer's calculations into music.

Other composers have tended to employ various other styles or influences. Terry Riley (b. 1935), for example, uses techniques described as "minimalist" or "systematic." In works such as "In C," "A Rainbow in Curved Air," or "Desert of Ice," he demonstrates ways of combining simple fragments in a highly repetitive manner, relying on group interaction and intuition to induce mental states. Words such as *psychedelic, illusionist, hallucinatory,* and *transcendental* are usually applied. Here the influence of music around the Pacific Rim is overwhelming. The music of the gamelan orchestras of Java and Bali, with their repetitive rhythms and melodies designed to induce certain mental states in the listener, has proved a fruitful source of inspiration for many musicians from Europe as well as North America. Steve Reich is another very prominent North American composer who employs these techniques. Perhaps one should not be surprised to find music of the Orient creating such powerful influence; the west coast of America is fairly remote from those centres of European culture that became the crucibles of many notions of musical art. The remoteness is both geographical and spiritual.

If nothing else the variety suggested by these brief descriptions of the works of some composers is undeniable. It is certainly far more diverse than one can find in any other century, from any point of view. It is easy to explain this variety as a reflection of the century itself. Again it is justifiable to state that no other century has seen such events on a worldwide basis as this one, and no other century has witnessed such extremes on such a large scale. It may be true that the very growth of uncertainty as a way of life in this century could hardly provide an atmosphere conducive to works of art that reflected order and continuity. All this does not make 20th century art in all its forms more easily understood or accepted by some.

If understanding is a prerequisite for acceptance then it is necessary to deal with some explanations. Explanations alone should not be regarded as a means of facilitating understanding of an individual artist's work, however. He deals in visual or auditory events that should explain themselves through sensory experience of them. Explanations are associated with the symbolism of words and concepts and can be helpful in overcoming a somewhat illogical bias favoring music of the eighteenth and nineteenth centuries, for example, but it is doubtful that they can be a real aid in understanding one's experience of art. However, a practising artist is concerned with "living" art, and to continue a dead cultural idiom is as unthinkable as the use of gunpowder would be to a modern general when he has nuclear weapons at his disposal in a war to the death. Here again, it must not be thought that an attempt is being made to present art as a progressive activity that gets better, or more effective. By way of naive illustration for the skeptical, liken the modern artist to a child when faced with a choice between a cowboy outfit and an electronic computer game. There is little doubt which he is likely to prefer nowadays, as parents will testify. After all, he sees movies such as *E.T* or *Return of the Jedi*, not *The Lone Ranger Rides Again*. There should be little convincing that a child who persists with cowboy outfits to the total exclusion of Pacman®, Intergalactica®, or Donkey Kong® would be regarded as a little weird. It would be surprising if there were no Stockhausens, Cages, Xenakises, etc. in today's world.

What is always particularly difficult for the general public is a new concept in "high" art, such as, for example, the notion of an art that is not particularly introspective and that is regarded by the artist as no more valuable than everyday objects, e.g. some art produced by the Dadaists or similar groups. The public is still trying to understand the eighteenth and nineteenth century notions of the transcendental qualities of music and, clearly, as a whole is not ready for this particular new idea. Along with ideas about the function and nature of art goes a certain type of content, and this century has, above all, produced a more revolutionary change in content than any other, and at a faster pace.

The Introduction of New Sounds in Art Music

Naturally if a composer subscribes to the view that art is not more important than everyday life, then he will not attempt to find sounds that are intended to "transport" the listener to mental states of "perfection." John Cage is just such a composer. Many of his works use sound in all its forms from everyday life, even silence. Even where a composer does not subscribe to such radically different views on the nature and function of art, there is evidence of equally drastic change. The orchestra is a case in point. Even the term is rather a loose one considering the types and combinations of instruments found in this century, in particular the enormous variety of tuned and untuned percussion instruments now in use.

It is perhaps misleading, however, to adumbrate developments in any one period of musical history in attempts to show radical change without reference to that history, and therefore, unfair to point out developments in this century without at least a mention of the startling (to the inexperienced ear) experiments of the past, if only to show that this century is not totally different in this respect. From Monteverdi in the early seventeenth century to Rameau in the eighteenth, and Wagner in the nineteenth, there is a long list of "daring" experimentalists in opera orchestration. This is not to mention the spin-off in the world of the symphonists, Mozart, Haydn, Beethoven, Berlioz, Mahler, and others. So when Bartock comes along with his extensions of string technique and additions of percussion instruments, we should hardly be surprised. Similarly Schoenberg's notion of colour melody is an acceptable kind of extension of developments in orchestration, yet it becomes a precursor of other ideas leading easily and naturally to electronic manipulation of sounds.

The important point is that in history just as in the contemporary scene, the additions and extensions to the orchestra, its constitution, and its playing techniques of various instruments were not just following on from what had gone before but were turning points in the view of some artists, from which there was no going back, only forward to newer idioms. The sonorities of Bartok's *Music for Strings, Percussion and Celeste* (first performed in 1937) are much more than a big step away from the kind of "impressionist" orchestrations of Debussy or Ravel. They represent a world of sound that became expanded in the works of later composers who were merely taking up from what they were born into. This is not to say that Bartok inspired such developments but rather that he exemplified them. There were others during the 1930s who were even more radical — Varèse for example. In the works of Bartok, however, one can see how different the 20th century really was. Bartok was traditional in his background and training, not overtly revolutionary as some were. His synthesis of older styles of construction, new sounds, and indigenous rhythms and melodies of eastern Europe produced an effect of enormous cultural complexity.

The third movement of *Music for Strings, Percussion and Celeste* contains some surprising sonorities and use of instruments. The mixture of timpani, xylophone, tam-tam, piano, celeste, bass drum, harp, and strings creates effects that can only be described as startling. The atmosphere generated by Bartok has been the inspiration for many composers of film scores, particularly horror films. The weirdness of the combination of glissandi on the harp and piano, glissandi motives on the celeste, and muted tremolo bowing on the strings has become associated in many people's minds with horror films, but the potential of such sonorities for further development did not go unnoticed. Gone is the use of tonal configurations in harmonic and contrapuntal explorations; here is an exploration of sound seeking a musical grammar based on different laws of syntax from those of tonality.

The same can be said of Edgard Varèse's "Ionisation," first heard in New York, in 1933. In this case the communications explosion referred to took more immediate effect, for during the 1930s the work was recorded on a 78-rpm disc by New Music Records. Thus a performance was available for a much wider audience, and no longer did the composer have to rely solely on someone's imperfect understanding of notation. Observations by artists who were strongly affected by Varèse indicate the impact of his ideas. For example, Earle Brown wrote:

> Virginia Woolf slowed up time and James Joyce almost stopped time. Joyce was exploring a situation in depth in a density kind of way, rather than horizontally, which was what Varèse was doing by observing the sheer fact of the sonic objects' reality which he constructed. He wanted

the sounds to just sit there, and have people listen in to the sounds. (Julius, 1981, p. 275)

The invention of new terms such as *world-opening* illustrates the influences of Varèse on various listeners. It is this idea of opening up sensibilities to all possible types of experience that characterizes the avant-garde of this century. It is not that older concepts in music are outmoded so much as inadequate to convey ideas where the search is for breadth, depth, and width. The listener who has experienced the "world-opening" sounds of Varèse listens to Wagner, or Mahler, or even Beethoven for very different reasons than those relating to "Ionisation." These historical figures are associated with concepts of fine feelings, sentimentally, or nobility; Varèse is associated with an openness of perceptual functioning that concerns knowing and understanding on levels far different from those of the nineteenth century consciousness.

In this latter case the rediscovery of Greek concepts of artistic meaning was influential, and discussion was about what, in qualitative terms, music meant. Thus Hanslick (*see* Chapter 2) argued about the precision with which music could evoke specific feelings, and the idea that music was a means of concretizing inner feelings or sentiments became firmly established. Wollheim, however (*see* Chapter 2), made a significant point by stating that we match our own feelings at a particular moment with those which seem to be present in some work of art. Thus if we feel particularly sentimental or overemotional, then we can listen to Wagner or Rachmaninov and find a musical vehicle for our feelings in their harmonies, melodies, and use of instruments. The interesting point is that if we do not feel particularly emotional, what does their music then mean to us? If, instead of listening to the composers mentioned, or similar ones, a listener in such an emotional state listened to Varèse or Cage, would he be able to read off similar emotional states to match his own? The answer must be a firm no, if only because we have been conditioned by the media to relate emotion to certain types of musical sounds.

Part of the motivation of some artists today is a desire to escape such associations of meaning with sound in favour of a more sensuous level of perceiving the qualities of the sound more for their own sake. The nineteenth century proclivity towards the affective favoured sounds like a slow sonorous melody on a cello, a penetrating passage on the horn, a sweet, emotional sweep of the violins, etc. These are the elements of sound that to the romantic mind provided the means of linking a state of perfection with the imperfect human condition; these sounds, therefore, had to awaken sentiments that fitted in with such aesthetic notions. The sounds of Cage's *First Construction in Metal* can have no such function. Written in 1939 in Seattle, he employs what to a nineteenth century symphonist would be a most unlikely collection of music-producing materials. Included are orchestral bells, thundersheets, a piano played in various unorthodox ways, a twelve-gong gamelan, cowbells, Japanese temple gongs, car brake drums, anvils, Turkish and Chinese cymbals, muted gong, water gong, i.e. a gong capable of suspension in water to alter the sound, and tam-tam. Conventional notations are used to denote the rhythms, but the effect on the listener is far from conventional. This is in fact, a step towards the "all-sound" music Cage referred to a few years before its composition. In other works, he has in fact used any sound, from traffic noises, to people's conversations, or even various combinations of different broadcasts from a number of radio stations.

One of the most prolific and influential composers today is Karlheinz Stockhausen. His works range from the use of conventional instruments such as the piano, full orchestra, various combinations of percussion, keyboard, and orchestral instruments, to electronic manipulations and generation of sounds both live and on prepared tape. He suggests that "it is necessary to listen to every detail" (Stockhausen, 1963, p. 63) of the sounds created so as to understand. This relates to his early works for piano and gives an indication of the role he expects in the listener, a role concerned with information theory applications to defining musical meaning and the significance of redundancy in musical expectation (*see* Meyer, 1956). In tonal music the amount of redundancy, i.e. repetition of tonal configurations, contributes to the building of expectations concerning the next sound, and it is the fulfilling or otherwise of these expectations that gives the music meaning. Stockhausen, in contrast, is presenting music that has no redundancy, no repetition, and therefore different criteria have to apply. The more redundancy, the less the information content, and deliberately, some music of Stockhausen can have very high or even maximum information content.

Consequently he requires the listener to listen to every detail of the sound, and it is this detail that supplies meaning. There is none of the kind of expectation building found in tonal music; every sound is a "world of meaning in itself." Here there are implications for musical structure as well as content, but for the moment we are concerned with the use of instruments, however interconnected form, content, and instrumentation become.

Among the less obviously radical, comparatively, of Stockhausen's use of sounds is the way he induces new types of sound from the piano in his compositions for that instrument during the 1950s. He requires the pianist to develop new techniques of performance so as to have at his disposal a wide range in dynamics, rhythm, and pitch, on a level never before attempted for the instrument. In dynamics, for example, he requires several different levels to be played simultaneously within a chord. In a four-note chord each note might be ascribed a different dynamic, e.g. *ff, p, mp,* and *pp,* to be played by four fingers on one hand. This is clearly a very difficult task for the pianist and equally difficult for the listener. There is some doubt whether such is physically possible to play, particularly at some of the high pitches Stockhausen requires for it. Similarly the use he makes of extremes in pitch, notes sometimes seven octaves apart, played simultaneously with differing dynamics, is theoretically attractive but practically almost impossible because of the physical characteristics of sound produced by the piano. A low note on the piano, for example, can be very difficult to produce at a *p* level compared with an *f* level for a very high note. However, despite the problems, dynamics are a significant part of the musical experience. As an illustration of this, in Piano Piece no. 1, (1953) at bar 20, there is a six-note chord spanning 5 octaves. The lowest note, B flat, is nearly two octaves below the bass stave and marked *ff.* The highest note is A above the treble stave, and marked *fff.* In the middle there is a treble G sharp marked *p,* an F sharp in the bass marked *ff,* and a low G in the bass stave marked *pp.* All these notes sound together. An even more extreme example can be seen at bar 11. Here the pitch range is only 2 octaves, but these are placed at the top of the treble stave upwards. A nine-note chord is to be struck with dynamics ranging from *fff* down to *p,* and as the chord dies notes are released in turn, leaving only the four highest. In retrospect it is easy to see from this early work why Stockhousen went into electronic music. The kind of control he requires over dynamics and note lengths is much easier to obtain using electronic controls than manual.

He stretches the use of the pedal to similar limits. In Piece no. 8 he specifies six different ways of affecting the sound by means of the pedal. In total, including the pedal instructions he specifies thirteen ways of playing notes, including staccato, "depressing the key silently," "depressing the key for the duration indicated." In this way he is creating the elements of a significant amount of new and diverse information to present to the listener. His purpose is concerned with establishing a new musical language which will be explained below.

Works such as *Momente* and *Gruppen* use enormously varied forces of instruments and voices in innovatory structural procedures. Perhaps the comparatively restrained resources of a work such as *Nr. 12 Kontakte* might serve to indicate something of the range of the new world of sound created by a mixture of percussion and prepared electronic music. Dating from 1960, the work employs a variety of wood instruments: African wood drums, marimbaphone, tom-toms with plywood glued in place of the membrane, a guero fixed to a stand, a hanging rattle consisting of twelve vertically suspended bamboo claves, a carillon of wood chimes, two woodblocks, and a bundle of small Indian bells suspended from a woodblock. A similar array of metal instruments is required, including thirteen antique cymbals, a small tam-tam, a hihat cymbal, a large cymbal, four cowbells, a larger tam-tam and gong, and various drums such as a bongo turned upside down, a side drum with snares, tom-toms, and a piano. The second version of *Kontakte* is for two instrumentalists (percussion and pianist) and the four-track prepared tape. Stockhausen explains in the score:

> This version is intended for performances in halls that offer the possibility of instrumental performance and, simultaneously, playback of the 4-track tape over 4 groups of loudspeakers (at left, front, right of the stage . . . etc.).(p. 1)

Harvey (1974) explains the content of the tape portion in which

> sounds were made after a long period in which Stockhausen analysed the acoustical structures of percussion sounds, by impulse generator, filter, reverberator and ring modulator . . . Thus "contact" can be made between instrumental and electronic sound although extremely sensitive performers are required — the piano especially, can easily be too loud etc. . . . (p. 88)

The work of Stockhausen, as much as that of any other composer, illustrates a highly integrated approach to organising sound, which sometimes requires electronic controls to produce the desired effect. The contrast and range in dynamics employed in the piano pieces is difficult to achieve and hear because of the limitations of the instrument. As Stockhausen himself pointed out in a lecture in Cambridge, England, in 1971, the use of electronic controls over sound was a logical step forward for him in his quest for structures that used all the elements of sound and required listeners to listen actively for every detail. With electronic controls he could jump from extreme to extreme in any parameter at the touch of a switch or button. Also, he could manipulate any parameter of sound, including envelope, and dynamic distribution among partials, as well as techniques of amplitude modulations, frequency modulations, ring modulation, etc.

The range possible is infinite, and the great problem facing the composer becomes that of choice as this music moves towards the atomization of sound and away from the clear pitch and its concomitant products melody, harmony, and tonal structures. This is the very problem today, for people tend to listen to music such as that by Varèse or Bartok or Stockhausen, etc., in the same way that they have been conditioned to listen to nineteenth century music or music of this century that has the same affective content. When they find that there is no emotional melody played on a cello or horn, no crescendo to whip up feelings, or no recognizable cadences with dissonances that pull at heart strings as they wait for their resolution, then they have no terms of reference to apply.

Nothing could be further from such nineteenth century concepts than a work such as John Cage's *Construction in Metal*. Cage explains:

> Since Arnold Schoenberg had impressed upon me the structural function of tonality I felt the need of finding some structural means adequate to composing for percussion. This led me eventually to a basic re-examination of the physical nature of sound. Sounds, including noises, it seemed to me, had four characteristics (pitch, loudness, timbre, and duration), while silence had only one (duration). I therefore devised a rhythmic structure based on the duration, not of notes, but of spaces in time . . . It is analogous to Indian Tala (rhythmic method), but it has the Western characteristic of a beginning and an ending. (Kostelanetz, 1978, p. 127)

Now many composers are using computors linked with synthesizers to calculate and determine the elements of sound to be employed.

Some reference has already been made to the impact of different ethnic cultures on the Western world. Clearly, many composers are responding to influences of the exotic (to the Western ear) sounds of ethnic music of all types. Various examples of string, wind, and percussion instruments present a bewildering variety of uses and sounds across the world. The Japanese Koto, or thirteen-string zither as we might call it, is played in a manner that produces a totally different sound from its European counterpart. The Persian santur, a kind of dulcimer, has a sound again totally different from anything from another country. The various string instruments of the lute type found the world over have superficial similarities, but their sounds are fascinating testimony to the effects of acculturation in producing diverse habits. They range from the primitive one-string kalandin from French Guinea, where a gourd is used as a resonator, to a sape from Sarawak, a two- or three-stringed boat-shaped instrument, and to the Chinese p'-p'a, which has four strings and must be played by a performer with long fingernails. Similarly, the variety of wind instruments is considerable. The saunay from the Philippines is a double reed instrument with a body fashioned from a wound leaf, and it is used for ceremonies such as weddings. Another double reed instrument is the zurna from Tunisia, but found widely in Asia. Many types of straight and transverse flutelike instruments can be found, as well as horns made from animal horn. Similarly the variety of drums is almost limitless. There is a slit drum, which is a hollow piece of wood with a slit in it placed on the legs and beaten with two small wooden beaters. These can be found in many sizes. Another type altogether is the Kundy drum from Papua, New Guinea, looking a bit like bongo drums. A drum of an extremely colourful look and sound is the kondang batangan found in the gamelan orchestras of southern Asia. The list is seemingly endless, and these few examples will suffice to indicate the variety.

In Western culture the advent and growth of jazz have introduced an instrumental combination that is now a kind of musical institution. This is the combination of rhythm section, comprising one player on drums, cymbals, and various percussion instruments; keyboard, either acoustic or electric piano; one or more melody instruments ranging from trumpet, saxophone, clarinet, trombone, etc.; and a bass player, originally a string bass but often now a bass guitarist. Such a combination lends itself to the improvised structures of jazz in all its forms. It has flexibility in terms of combinations, as well as a balance in sound between the elements of rhythmic backing, a bass part, and improvised melodic parts above. There is also scope for each individual player to improvise a solo spot.

New Notations for New Sounds

The foregoing brief survey is by no means intended to be fully representative and certainly is not exhaustive. The intention is to awaken interest in the great variety of sounds that now form part of the musical pactices in many cultures the world over, which have been used in works by composers in this century. Only closer examination of scores, listening to recordings, and attending concerts can provide a full picture of what is happening in music today. For music education purposes such exposure is necessary. However, having provided this brief outline it becomes clear that with the emphasis on new sounds there must be a corresponding development in notations for the sounds. Notations, as with all aspects of musical art, are continually developing and adapting in response to new ideas from composers. Historically this can be observed over long time spans, from ninth century neumonic notation, to medieval mensuration, to modern metric notations using the five-lined stave, etc. As long as instruments did not use sounds too far outside the capabilities of the human voice, the use of the stave was adequate. In this century, however, all possible combinations of auditory experience are considered available for music. Consequently, new notations have had to be invented. There is no uniform practice apparent, but it is possible to see a few types of notations capable of classification of sorts.

Each composer has tended to invent his own notations to suit his own purpose and has resorted to verbal explanations of their meaning. In this type any symbol is appropriate provided it has the required explanation for the performer. In such a situation it is not surprising to find almost anything used for symbolic purposes. Lu-

ciano Berio, in *Circles*, uses "frames,", rectangles containing a mixture of conventional and nonconventional musical symbols. The
frame itself may be a part of the information to the performer in
parameters other than time — its principal function. Sometimes a
part of the frame has a thicker line denoting louder sounds at that
point. Where pitch precision is not a factor and the composer requires movements up or down, it is common to find some point of
reference, perhaps a horizontal line, and a number of shapes
describing pitch movement around it. Ligeti in his work *Volumina*
writes a passage for organ pedal that is notated by a thick undulating
line moving up and down between two horizontal lines representing
the pitch extremes of the pedals. Penderecki requires his tenors to
whistle (as high as possible) in *Dimensionen der Zeit und der Stille*. He
graphically describes his intentions by means of one undulating line
around a horizontal reference line. At one point he indicates a sudden dip in pitch followed by a sudden sharp rise, which looks like a *V*
(*see* Karkoshka, 1972).

Rhythm or time structures have become so radically different
from anything preexisting this century that conventional time signa-
tures and note lengths are wholly inadequate in many works. Solutions to finding notations are just as varied as the situations that
require notations. Some composers use a grid, or a graphlike background, for placing symbols, and each square on the graph represents some time span expressed in seconds or minutes. Morton
Feldman's *In Search of an Orchestration* uses this kind of grid system,
and each square in the grid lasts a predetermined length of time. Inside the squares are a wide variety of conventional and nonconventional symbols, the meanings of which are explained at the
beginning of the score. Other composers use loose time controls in
that they require a certain length of time for a number of events to
interact, so there may be several instruments or taped sounds occurring in random or predetermined order during the allotted time
span. This span is indicated by vertical lines at the appropriate place
in the score. An example of this is R. Murray Schafer's *Threnody for
Youth Orchestra, Youth Choir, Five Narrators and Electronic Music*. Here he
stretches the use of the stave to new limits, where it is merely a reference point in providing free notations. The structure and overall
durations within the piece are determined either by the narrated text
or by the prepared tape of electronic sounds. The performers take

their cues from these two sources.

In this work the players are intended to be school children, and they are asked to read from the full score so that they may "follow the performance and prepare for their cues." In the preface to the score Schafer explains:

> A careful discussion of the score with the performers followed by sectional rehearsals would be desirable to work matters out. A few questions are left, purposely, unanswered in the score. Here the performers must take matters into their own hands and work out suitable solutions.

The main reference points for the performers are the time frames expressed in seconds. Some are precise, like the passage for trumpets suggesting a loose kind of fanfare in the indeterminate pitch notations used, but rhythmically made to conform to four quarter notes in a bar, where each quarter note lasts for one second. Others are less so, as in another passage for trumpets where a fanfare of precisely notated pitches becomes a long held cluster lasting "approximately 8 seconds." Many of the time placings of instrumental interjections during the sounds of the tape or of other instruments are mere placings on the score, and their exact point of entry has to be decided through discussion, as indicated in the preface.

In electronic music, duration is, inevitably, expressed numerically indicating lengths in minutes and seconds. Precise controls can be exercised in the use of prepared tapes by means of relating tape length to its movement in the playback time. The use of time frames, or grids, or some kind of vertical line division down the score is fairly universal in electronic scores to denote duration.

Other parameters of music tend to be notated in similar fashion. This in itself is an interesting fact since in the past pitch and rhythm notations dominated and were supplemented by a few other notations for dynamics and musical structures such as phrasing, etc. Today the elements of music are not overshadowed by pitch and rhythm concepts and so notations are not so predominantly concerned with them. Dynamic levels, for example, tend to be indicated through size of symbol in some scores; the larger the size the louder the sound. In Stockhausen's *Telemusik* the sounds of a Japanese drum (*mokugyo*) are denoted by black spots diminishing in size as the sound of the individual drum beats get softer. A cluster of notes played on a number of instruments is often denoted by a thick black line, the length of which indicates the duration of the sound. In Earle Brown's *4 Systems*, for piano or other instruments, all the elements of the structure are illustrated graphically. Produced in 1954, this piece explores the whole piano keyboard. Sounds are represented by lines. Thick lines are loud, thin ones are soft. Lines placed high are high sounds, and those placed low are correspondingly low. Duration is related to length of line. Vertical combinations of lines indicate combined sounds of different duration, loudness, and pitch. Brown wanted to indicate to the performer something of the "spiritual" quality of the work as he realised the score. Since the score is entirely objective in its deployments of lines as described, it was necessary to write an explanation:

> . . . to have elements exist in space as an infinitude of directions from an infinitude of points in space . . . to work (compositionally and in performance) to right, left, back, forward, and all points in between . . . the score being a picture of this space at one instant, which must always be considered as unreal and/or transitory . . . a performer must set this all in motion (time), which is to say, realize that it is motion and step into it . . . either sit and let it move or move through it at all speeds . . . It is primarily intended that performances be made directly from this graphic "implication" (one for each performer) and that no further defining of events, other than the agreement as to total performance time, takes place. (Earle Brown, *4 Systems*, 1954)

This has moved a long way from the deliberately affective compositions of the nineteenth century. Here we can see a vision of a kind of music preexisting in space and time, and the composer merely outlines a possible method for the performer to find a way to step into an already existing auditory world through the notations. The onus is, therefore, placed upon the performer to succeed in this task. The type of perceptual functioning required of the listener is on at least two levels: one is concerned with the peripheral sensations of basic elements of sounds, the other is with a mystical awareness of another dimension of auditory experience in time and space. Intuition plays a big part in deciding whether or not either the performer or the listener has succeeded in first finding a way to step into the already existing world and then in communicating with each other.

Not all scores require the performer to attempt communications of this sort using a rather imprecise method of notation. Some specify in detail both the pitch and rhythm parameters and other details but, because of some overall structural procedure, are contained within time frames, or grids.

New Concepts of Musical Structure

Musical structure is another more significant area developed in music today. Its essence is sometimes reflected in the notations employed. For example some composers, wishing for greater flexibility for a variety of reasons, do not specify any elements of sounds, merely indicating the actions by means of some verbal text. Some of these scores are mystical in origin, such as Stockhausen's *Aus den seiben Tagen*. This piece contains "ideas for improvisation" and came into being as explained by Harvey (1974):

> During seven days in early May 1968 Stockhausen shut himself up, ate nothing, meditated much. The result was a book of fifteen brief sets of instructions couched, this time, not in practical language, but in suggestive evocative language which has distilled what he wants performers to do. (p. 113)

One example is "Verbindung" ("Connections"):
"Play a vibration in the rhythm of your body
Play a vibration in the rhythm of your heart"
which goes on to list breathing, thinking, intuition, enlightenment, the universe, and finally suggests they are mixed freely and to "leave enough silence between them." Cott (1974) cites the composer's reference to this kind of score and musical product in a lecture Stockhausen gave in Vienna to music publishers. He suggested that the possibilities of "a kind of psychic music in which a composer would instruct performers telepathically" are of great interest to him. There are many other types of verbal scores in existence, the most extreme, perhaps, being those of Cornelius Cardew in *Nature Study Notes*. Many have the appearance of games rather than any serious attempts of the types listed previously to communicate lofty ideas or concepts. One, for example, merely shows a packet of cigarettes and suggests that they be passed around, indicating more of a Dadaist approach to music.

Other types of "free" structures are more prescribed in the notations for musical events, even if the total structure is left open. Stockhausen's Piano Piece no. XI consists of nineteen groups of notes, or structures. Each tends to vary considerably in length and detail. These structures, or groups as the composer calls them, are printed randomly across the large sheet of paper of the score. The performer looks at random and begins to play any group that catches his attention. He chooses his own tempo, dynamic level, and type of attack. After playing the group he reads the instructions concerning tempo, dynamics, and attack that follow it, then chooses another group. This process is repeated until all nineteen groups have been played. The chances of the same performance being repeated are astronomical (over 10^{17}), and in the score it is suggested that the piece be played twice at each performance.

Stockhausen explains in the score, "The field structure of a large form like this will become clearer, naturally, when it is played several times in succession." In statistical terms the language potential of a piece such as this is a function of the total number of possible variants to ordering the nineteen groups (over 10^{17}) and the amount of information each group contains in terms of pitch, dynamics, durations, tempo, attacks, and their combinations. It is in fact an entire language system in itself. Redundancy of the type described by Meyer would be almost impossible to achieve even with many playings to familiarise the listener. It is clearly a challenge to our perceptual functioning generally. The response required cannot be explained in terms that apply to traditional concepts of tonal music, where repetition and its consequent redundancy and expectation building are the main perceptual and conceptual referents.

Many other composers use this kind of random ordering of musical events. Earle Brown and Pierre Boulez are but two of them. However, the idea of building structures by concentrating attention on the detail of each event, rather than how they interrelate, is novel. The longitudinal structures of tonal music require an understanding of thematic, key-centered, and developmental ideas that are progressive and linked in terms of tonal relationships. The structures of many composers' works today require no such links to be made. Instead, with the whole logic system of tonality abandoned, other criteria have emerged. One of the earliest of this century was that of serialism, developed by Schoenberg and his pupils. The main principle of this system is that all notes are equally important, whatever their order of appearance. There is no keynote as such, and consequently there can be no feeling of key, or tonality in the traditional sense, and therefore no building of tonal tensions for subsequent relief. It must be added that composers today can still build and relieve tensions but by other means than those of tonial logic: building such in timbre and dynamics is one that is well tried.

In a century where things have moved so fast it is perhaps surprising that serialism took so long to take hold. However, artistic activity went into a decline during the Second World War and immediately before it, largely because of Nazi persecution, and it wasn't until after the war ended that it all started up again and the ideas of Schoenberg and others deported from Europe began to be explored. Messiaen, after spending some years in a prisoner of war camp, returned to Paris and began teaching composition. He was particularly interested in serialism, though not exclusively so. He used many different methods of structuring a piece and ordering events within. In 1949 he wrote a piano piece entitled "Mode de Valeurs et D'intensites" (Mode of durations and dynamics). It is regarded as a serial work in which he organises elements of pitch, using his own modal techniques, durations, and dynamics, and relates these elements using number sequences. He uses twelve different durations and twelve different types of attack. He developed his own language forms in music, which ranged from a mixture of various modal scales he produced, to Eastern rhythmic and melodic patterns, and bird song. One of his pupils, Pierre Boulez, took Messiaen's serialist teachings further and produced a number of works in the early 1950s that are based on these ideas. Whittall (1977) quotes from Boulez's Darmstadt lectures on structure:

> The world of music today is . . . one where structural relationships are not defined once and for all according to absolute criteria, but are organised instead according to varying schemata . . . this world has arisen from the expansion of the idea of the series.

Whittal (1977) explains further that the extremely short "Bagatelles" for string quartet by Webern (opus 9) brought something quite new, in the opinion of Boulez, who, in 1952, wrote what he called a "totalitarian" serialist composition. This was "Structure la" for two pianos, and he acknowledged the influence of Messiaen and his "Mode de Valeurs et D intensites." The atomization of musical sounds evident in Webern clearly had a big impact on Boulez, and it must be remembered that Webern's "Bagatelles" date from before the First

World War.

From the above comments it should be clear that tonal forms such as sonata, fugue, and simpler structures such as binary and ternary can no longer have the validity for composers that they enjoyed in the eighteenth and nineteenth centuries. Then tonality, not serialism, was the fashion, and tonal tensions and relationships between keys were the bases for structures. Serialism poses entirely different problems, and entirely different structures result. There can be no simple formula for serialist structure, such as some musicologists would have us believe there is for tonal structures, in particular sonata form. It is enlightened music teaching that assumes that sonata form cannot be reduced to the simplistic exposition, development, and recapitulation formula that generations of music students have been brought up on. From a distance in time it is so tempting to reduce to what are perceived as basic concepts, and few writers on music in the eighteenth or nineteenth centuries spent much space on form, certainly not as many as do today.

We are able to get a clearer notion of the complexity and variety of forms today, and not just in serial works, if only because composers feel the need to explain and justify more than ever before. Despite this it is assumed that music of the past is easier to understand than music of today; that sonata form is easy, fugue is easy, opera is easy, all because of the retrospective ability to reduce to the simplistic those concepts associated with tonality. As anyone knows who has bothered to look beyond a few well known models of such concepts, this is far from the truth. The variety of treatment found in all these tonal structures is extremely wide. This is important to realise in looking at structure in this century so as to dispel the myth that music is more complex today than in the past. Unfamiliarity of pitch movement, i.e. nontonal, therefore nonmelodic, or of rhythm, i.e. nonmetrical, therefore difficult to identify patterns, should not be confused with complexity. Many of the serialist works sound more complex than they actually are for reasons of unfamiliarity rather than actual complexity. In many ways it can be demonstrated that some are more logical and less complex than some of their tonal ancestors from another age. It must also be pointed out that logic in musical structure is something inherent in the individual work rather than something drawn from the wider fields of logical discourse, whatever the period, content, or idiom. There is no more a simple formula for understanding the motet, the symphony, or the mass than there is for serialist compositions.

A brief look at Boulez's "Structure la" will indicate the kind of problems and solutions inherent in serialism. He uses a pitch series from the Messiaen work referred to previously in homage to his teacher. For rhythm he uses the thirty-second note (demisemiquaver) as the basic unit, and the series comprises multiples of from one to twelve of this unit. Thus he has twelve pitches and twelve note lengths from which to form his basic series. He prepares two tables of numbers, which present a variety of ways of ordering the sequence one to twelve. These tables are derived from methods vertically aligning different orders of the note row and substituting numbers. He forms a similar range of twelve dynamic levels, from *ppp* through to *ffff*, which correspond to numbers one to twelve. Thus he has twelve pitches, twelve durations, and 12 dynamic levels, each of which can be substituted by its allotted number between one to twelve. Had he used a computer he could have made available all the theoretically possible orders of the numbers one to twelve. In this way he would have had up to 479,001,600 different orders of the number series. The problems of choice would then have assumed gigantic proportions. In his search for homogeneity, however, he limited his choices to the tables referred to. In the fourth parameter, timbre, Boulez numbers different modes of attack on the piano from one to twelve but leaving out numbers four and ten. He requires only ten modes of attack for his structural purposes. The difficulties of playing and hearing such detail have already been exposed.

The big problem of the piece as far as homogeneity is concerned is that of linking all the four elements. Boulez uses the two tables for this. Here we can see the advantage of using the tables. Each is a twelve by twelve box of numbers that can be read down, across, and diagonally, thus facilitating random choices of these possibilities in a visual manner. The entire piece is woven out of what Ligeti (1960) calls serial threads, that is orderings of the original rows or their variants related to two tables of numbers. The individual threads are united to form "bundles," (1960) and the two pianos each have a "bundle running" simultaneously. There are fourteen sections within which, because of the operations of the number series referred to, the content is automatically decided upon. The desire of Boulez to be as homogeneous as possible in his "totalitarian" serialism is confronted with problems. For example, the duration series (as Ligeti points out) is additive whereas the pitch series is proportional, and there is a difference in quality between the transpositions of the pitch series, where the interval relationships remain the same, and the permutations of the duration series, which are not so organic, merely mechanical.

At about the same time Stockhausen was writing his first serial works. His approach, while similar in some respects, resulted in a different type of product. His first "Piano Piece," one of a set of four, was first performed at the 1954 Darmstadt Summer School and was the prototype of a structure made up of what he calls "groups." These are not the same as the bundles referred to in the works of Boulez. Moreover it appears that Stockhausen has attempted to reduce the significance of the serial structure and automatic procedures resulting from the working out of number sequences in favour of an overview of the impact of sounds. At least this is what he appears concerned with in his retrospective views on the work. He reports optimistically that at its first performance the audience, consisting mainly of musicians, responded by whistling their own improvised sounds (he calls them groups) in the silences between the "groups" of his work. A group is defined by the pauses that precede and follow it. The pause draws its character from the groups that surround it. Stockhausen (1963) explains:

> One of the ways into the music is to pay particular attention to when and how the pauses occur, and how relatively long or quiet they are felt to be. This depends upon the group both before and after; whether the sounds are dense, or thinly textured and so on. The aim is to experience in these sudden silences, or gradual pauses, as much as we experience in the notes themselves . . . whoever senses this experiences the music much more deeply as a result. (p. 19)

This is apparently a rather different approach to the attempt at "totalitarian" serialism of Boulez. Stockhausen is suggesting a stage further removed from mere perception of the result of automatic procedures and the consequent detail of sound. He talks of a "quality of experience of a higher order" and suggests that "it is necessary to listen to every detail rather than to try and relate to some vast preordained scheme." He does refer to the detail, and this is the important point. "A group has an atomized structure" he points out (p. 63), and in all these statements he is proposing theoretical relationships based upon atomization of musical sounds. Thus from the detail he suggests the total structure is perceived.

The structure of the first "Piano Piece" can be explained on both a macro and a micro level. On the former level there are thirty-six groups, with six series of groups. Each series, therefore, has six groups in it. A group is either one or two bars and comprises a musical event with the perceived characteristics in all parameters of sound making up its nature. These characteristics are described by Stockhausen in terms of loudness, attack, pitch level, note combinations, pitch movement, and rhythmic structures. Furthermore he talks of correspondences between groups. These are not mere similarities, although they can be, but are more complex types of relationship, some associated with proportion, some with pitches, order of notes, etc.

On the micro level there is a great deal of information concerning both the structure and method of composition. The numbers one to six play a highly significant role throughout. Each group, for example, lasts a number of quarter notes (crotchets), and within each series, each group is assigned a number from one to six. In the first series we get the following: Bar 1 = group 1 = 5/4; Bar 2 = group 2 = 2/4; Bar 3 = group 3 = 3/4; Bar 4 = group 4 = 3/8; Bar 5 = group 5 = 4/4; Bar 6 = group 6 = 6/4. Thus the number order for this series is 5;2;3;1;4;6. These are proportional relationships expressed in quarter notes as follows: Series (1) 523146; Series (2) 365421; Series (3) 264315; Series (4) 146253; Series (5) 651432; Series (6) 135264. Clearly the use of some kind of source for the various order of the numbers one to six is essential. Boulez used his own tables. It is not clear how Stockhausen arrived at his choices, but there is a total of 720 to choose from, and it is possible that he had a computer printout of all the possibilities or he worked them out manually and chose them at random. Pitches are organized using this series one to six. The twelve note of the chromatic scale are divided into two hexachords, the first middle C to F, and the second F sharp to B. Each pitch within a hexachord is assigned a number one to six. The complete row appears in the piece thirty-six times, each time subdivided into the two hexachords. There are some errors in the appearances, for example at the fifth appearance where the second hexachord has two B flats (or note 5 in the series), or in the 26th appearance where again in the second hexachord there is no

F sharp (or note number 1). He used similar procedures to organise rhythm and types of attack on the piano.

The idea of groups was developed further by Stockhausen. As composers gradually began to tire of the automatic workings out of serial structures and move towards those which enabled greater personal controls at all levels, or even those which relied on intuition from the performer, other methods of determining content took over. Moment form is the most important new form that Stockhausen developed out of these early works. In this form a moment is an independent musical event,

> individual and self-regulated, and able to sustain an independent existence. The musical events do not take a fixed course between a determined beginning and an inevitable ending, and the moments are not merely consequents of what precedes them and antecedents of what follows; rather the concentration is the NOW . . . the composer is no longer in the position of beginning from a fixed point in time and moving forwards from it; rather he is moving in all directions within a materially circumscribed world." (Smalley, 1974, p. 25)

The most representative work of this type is *Momente* (1964). The work has some serialist elements and is not indeterminate, but that "any number and combination of Moments can change position means that there is a very large number of possible forms;" (Whittall, 1977, p. 261). As Whittall states, it is moment form that has established Stockhausen's preeminence in avant-garde music today, and evidence of it can be seen in the early group form works.

Other writers than Whittall have commented on the central role of discontinuity in twentieth century music as opposed to that of progress and development in tonal music. This is perhaps a negative way of putting things, for the emphasis is not so much on discontinuity for its own sake but rather a focus on the immediacy of the present moment, which is going to be different from the next moment, and so on. This reflects changing views of life and the things that we imagine influence living. While not getting too deeply enmeshed in this topic, it is important to mention that the events of the early twentieth century, the slaughter of the Great War in particular, turned the optimistic nineteenth century belief in order and hierarchy into a profound disillusionment, and this was reflected in literature, visual art, and music. It was at this time, i.e. the first two decades of the century, that futurism in art of all kinds emerged.

With hindsight it is now possible to see certain trends emerging into definite artistic ideas in music. What began to most observers as mere anarchy in sound has become a viable artistic entity.

It was during the 1950s that ideas began to crystallise, and this has already been explained. But earlier composers had already used incipient moment forms: Debussy in *Jeux* (1913), for example. This work was the subject of lectures and articles by the Darmstadt composers, including Stockhausen, because they recognised principles of discontinuity in isolated "moments of sound," which stood on their own as comprising the structural logic of the work. Later writers notably Kramer (1981) have pointed out the same principles in Stravinsky's *Symphonies of Wind Instruments*. Kramer (1981) provides an analysis of the work to demonstrate this and explains:

> The techniques of this piece are both a culmination of Stravinsky's earlier methods and an anticipation of the radically non-linear procedures of a younger generation in whose music moments are truly independent both of each other and of an underlying progressive logic. (Kramer, 1981, p. 63)

The important point in Stravinsky's work is that he was able to "strip tonal sounds of their kinetic implications and freeze them in motionless nonprogressions" (p. 63). This is a particularly difficult concept because tonal elements will appear to move onwards in tonal progressions, and to write tonal sounds that do not move onwards, where each individual tonal element is an entity in itself, is indeed radical, particularly as the piece moves onward but, as Kramer points out, by "non-tonal means." If there is any kind of recognisable underlying trend in the twentieth century in music, this is it.

The use of individual, nonconnected in any organic or thematic sense, self-contained sections that together make up a piece of music has replaced the old concept of progression, linearity, and organic unity upon which all kinds of extramusical concepts could be "hung." This is not possible in moment form pieces because the listener is required to be himself, stripped of all his acquired learning about what music means, and respond to the immediate present sensation of sounds in all their parameters for a short while, and then as the next moment comes to expect something different. In fact, expecting something different rather than a progression does become the norm of expectancy in such music. The sensuality of sound that Debussy and Ravel expounded in their works has given way to become a much more complex structural concept with moment form.

Implicit in these ideas is a notion about awareness of the passage of time and its relationship with what happens in music. Messiaen was very much a leading figure for the Darmstadt group in the 1950s because of his ideas concerning structures; some are very much sectionalised moments in isolation. At some stage he was concerned with producing static harmony, that is harmony that does not progress. The organ piece "Le Banquet Celeste" is an early example, but there are passages here that can be described as progressing despite a general sense of stasis throughout. Robert Sherlaw Johnson explains:

> He (Messiaen) arrives at a position which is analogous to Eastern music because of his attitude to harmony as a static element. A sense of time, marked by an evolving texture, is fundamental to Bach and Beethoven, but it has always been Messiaen's aim to suspend the sense of time in music . . . in order to express the idea of the eternal — in which time does not exist — as distinct from the temporal. (Kramer, 1981, p. 66)

The way time passes has become an important concern in this kind of music. In historical music, where there was a sense of progression, time was a function of perception of the progression, and the listener was not so much aware of the uniqueness of each individual moment as of the overall unified goal of melody, harmony and counterpoint. For example, the "Tristan chords" require resolution into a sense of precise tonality and a particular key centre. It happens at the end of the opera when the dramatic denouement occurs. Time is thus suspended over long periods in a musical mechanical sense as our emotions are carried along the linear musical statement. The reverse occurs in listening to a piece in sectionised form. The listener is aware of each section, or moment; of its qualities, its nature, its effect. When it has finished it is necessary to become aware of the next moment and relate to it in the same manner. It follows that a moment can have any length of time from a few seconds to a number of minutes, though there is a perceptual limit to the amount of time we can concentrate on such "total" information content without it losing its impact. Moreover, it becomes necessary to use some proportions for determining structural content. Proportionality between moments is one of the most important features of the work of some composers; Stockhausen is one, and this has already been explained in relation to his first "Piano Piece."

A composer working in this kind of structural determinant is involved with musical concepts of a radically different nature from his counterpart in the eighteenth or nineteenth century. Today, musical composition involves not so much a knowledge of the development of tonality and all that implies, as it does a sense of understanding the nature of sound, the importance of every detail of musical content, the "openness" of content embracing all sounds and all facets of sounds, the significance of silence, the importance of perceptual awareness in the listener, the degree of concentration required to become aware of such detail, and the central notion of discontinuity to emphasize the present moment of attention rather than be carried along as in tonal music in a kind of linear logic of progression, which has no support in modern science as its basis. This is perhaps a most significant point, for composers of today are consciously relating their music to the contemporary laws of science. It could certainly be argued that composers of the past also related to their contemporary laws of science. It ought not be necessary to point out, however, the explosion of knowledge of the last few decades and the radical epistemological changes that have occurred over the last few hundred years. It follows, therefore, that Stockhausen, Varèse, Boulez, Cage, etc., are merely reflecting their world of existence in much the same way as did Monteverdi, Gluck, Mozart, Wagner, etc. The importance for music education lies in the nature of today's world of scientific knowledge and its impact on the arts, and therefore on the perceiver of artistic works. Music education needs to be concerned with these things at least as much as with perpetuation of mystique from past ages.

7

INNOVATION IN THE CLASSROOM

DURING the 1960s a reflection of some developments in contemporary music began to show itself in music classrooms in a number of countries. There exists some concrete evidence of this in the form of publications, but there is a bigger corpus of experience of teachers and students that has gone unrecorded. The published material is the only firm evidence, but it does represent the tip of the iceberg. It reflects a much wider range of activities practised by teachers working in relative isolation, grappling with new ideas formulated through their own musical and professional teaching experiences.

The writer, for example, while teaching in a large grammar school in central England during the mid 1960s began experimenting with sounds in music lessons. An important question is Why? There are two basic reasons: one is the observed effects of teaching traditional music skills of performance and listening in a traditional manner, and the other is exposure to works by contemporary composers and a growing puzzlement over why colleagues teaching in other subject areas such as language arts or visual art could freely use contemporary sources while music teachers felt a hidden pressure to ignore this obvious source of educational material. There were ample opportunities to hear live or even recorded contemporary works, but a chance encounter with a record of John Cage's *First Construction in Metal* as it lay on the shelves of the record collection in the local library was important. The experience of hearing such sounds provided a new focus and suggested many possibilities. As a consequence, during the following years general class music and activities by accomplished musicians in the school became concerned with experimental compositions for everyone, musicians and nonmusicians, each contributing what they could. All manner of materials were employed to produce sound, including conventional musical instruments, and many kinds of structures were tried. There was great enthusiasm from all concerned, and a new life seemed to be injected into classroom activity that, by comparison, had seemed moribund. One very interesting observation for the writer was the response of parents. At this grammar school it was extremely favourable. Nothing short of delight was expressed, even to the extent of one parent confessing that a recent concert with experimental music had helped make up her mind not to send her child to a fee-paying school because of the "wide range of musical activities of such an interesting nature." In this writer's opinion this is a revealing viewpoint from a parent at that time in England, before the introduction nationwide of comprehensive secondary schools. Clearly there was no hostility to experimental music in a grammar school; there was respect for the efforts of the staff and pupils. The same cannot be said for attitudes of parents subsequently as such schools became embroiled in the controversy over comprehensive schools, i.e. all-ability schools as opposed to the selective grammar schools. Experimental music came to be linked with the generally regarded educational sloppiness of the unpopular new comprehensive schools, which had replaced the old separate schools for different ability levels. In a debate over the value of new ideas in education it is not helpful to contaminate discussions with the kind of bias that characterised the controversy referred to. An interesting question remains: If the grammar schools had remained to develop experimental music in schools in England would it have still struggled for acceptance? It is important to view it objectively, free from the political subjectivity that has tended to surround it and other educational activities in the last two decades.

Subsequent discussion with teaching colleagues has shown that many were engaged in experimental music activities during the late 1960s and early 1970s. What was missing was an opportunity for exchange of ideas. This tended to give an impression to most that they were working alone as the inventor or, depending upon one's views in this matter, the perpetrator of something doubtful as far as traditional music education was concerned. In England during the 1960s the shadows of the great private schools hung over the state-maintained system, and schools tended to cling to nineteenth century ideas of competition between and within schools. Collaboration was, therefore, something talked about but rarely practised. In 1970, in London, there was a national conference held entitled Music for the Unwilling. A large attendance indicated high interest at least in the problems of teaching some music to the mass of children in schools. In the absence of any real coordination of activities, or leadership from any central authorities, personal anecdotal material is one vital source of information, however limited it may be in helping to describe the educational milieu in which music teachers worked as they attempted to make music a classroom activity at least equal to that of other subject areas in its contemporary appeal to the bulk of students who were not trying to emulate Beethoven, or Yehudi Menuhin, or some great conductor such as Toscanini.

It is only through published material that it is possible to see some tangible evidence of the scope of ideas being developed and practised. From the middle and late 1960s onwards there have been a number of short, stimulating publications that have helped to interest the next generation of teachers in experimental music in the classroom through disseminating information about the individual experiences of the authors.

Discounting the Summer Camps of John Cage in the United States and others of a much earlier date, one of the first situations whereby a composer was working with children, or students, on a regular basis in activities of an experimental nature was in southern England. This was in a small country grammar school where Peter Maxwell Davies was full-time teacher of music. In 1961 his work was given wide publicity through the televised performance of a new work specially composed for his students: *O Magnum Mysterium*. The work had medieval inspiration in both the music and the largely religious text and is a collection of vocal *a cappella* items and instrumental pieces, including an organ solo. Apart from this solo all the items were intended to be performed by children, either playing orchestral or percussion instruments or singing. It must be emphasized, however, that the performers were expected to have a good standard of competence; this was not "music for all." Here was a young composer exploring the techniques of composition and sharing the process with the students. *O Magnum Mysterium* was a public manifestation of the kind of daily contact between students and composer that was being established at the school. The vocal items explore Maxwell Davies's linear techniques whereby relatively simple chromatic lines are combined to form harmony. Each line is based upon the regular use of one or two intervals and could be sight-read by a student with competent school standards. The instrumental pieces combine various percussion and orchestral instruments in structures that allow for free improvisation and, in places, basic manipulations of simple movements such as loud and soft, short and long. Through such techniques Maxwell Davies encouraged his students to think about the compositional process, and while of not much help to those taking formal music examinations, they did provide a chance to address issues related to compositional procedures. A significant point in this context is that Maxwell Davies developed his experimental music in schools on a foundation of traditional music skills and traditional training in vocal and instrumental techniques. It did not, therefore, satisfy criteria for class music making, since such skills were something of a prerequisite for performance of his music. This meant that, generally, those students who derived the most from his work were the most musically committed and the most musically competent.

The situation described is a kind of apprenticeship whereby a master works with and through his apprentices, in this case the students. In musical history this was the normal way to be educated. Moreover, exploring the nature of music through experimentation with sounds is not new in concept, but in this case new in content and extent. The process has been written about by John Cage and others in the earlier decades of the post war period. It is, however, one thing to practise such ideas as an artist in society at large and quite another to attempt to establish such practises in an institution such as a school or college. This is important, for the publications that will be described here represent attempts to disseminate information about the individual writer's or project group member's personal experiences with students in experimental activities in music. They do not indicate the establishment of experimental music in schools. Even now, in 1983, "experimental" music is still regarded as "experimental"; it is by no means institutionalized in the sense of being accepted as a valid educational activity and has made few real inroads into the school music curriculum. It is important to examine both why this is so and whether an acceptable theoretical basis can be established for such music in the classroom. Of particular relevance is the distinction between activity for everyone, irrespective of levels of musical competence, and activity that, however experimental, can only really be attempted by those with some minimum level of musical competence. The activities of Peter Maxwell Davies are in the latter category while some of the activities yet to be described are in the former. It is this former category which has largely failed to gain substantial support educationally and musically. Whether this is because of its fragmentary nature, its ill-defined conceptual basis, bias in attitudes towards it, or all three in some combination is a question that needs addressing.

It is necessary to emphasize that the experimental music being practised in schools during the 1960s and 1970s reflected ideas and attitudes that had currency in the world of practising contemporary musicians. The ideas of avant-garde composers were disseminated in both performances of new music and writings about music. The isolation of educational music from both musicians and educationists resulted in less than encouragement for those who attempted to practise new methods in schools.

Nevertheless there have been an increasing number of publications on the topic. They range from short books to individual pieces or projects for "untrained" children. This is the real attraction for the school music teacher faced with a total school population who have "music" on their timetables. While it would be true to say that the movement grew partly out of individual, personal dissatisfaction with the observed effects of traditional methods of teaching traditional historical music to the mass of increasingly unwilling students, whose music lessons had always had the ring of an entertainment period rather than serious work, it must be added that there were also strong positive reasons associated with a genuine interest in the excitement of contemporary musical activities. What has tended to be lacking, however, is a cogently argued educational reason for experimental music in the classroom beyond superficial statements about creativity or integration of subjects within a curriculum. Also, to state that this is what is happening in contemporary music has not given such activities educational validity in the opinion of many more traditionally minded music educators, who are, nevertheless, very much aware of the problems facing music education. It should be apparent that the activities of some contemporary musicians do not enjoy universal approval largely because of the legacy of historical attitudes and the conceptual nonsynchronisation between public tastes and activities of artists referred to in earlier chapters.

There is without doubt a twofold educational purpose behind the use of experimental music in schools: One is to bring the work of contemporary musicians into the classroom, and the other is to involve all children, not just the musically inclined and educated, in acts of music making, both performance and composition, at a level of intellectual and physical functioning commensurate with their ability and their work in other subjects. The acquisition of traditional musical skills, predominately related to pitch and rhythm, is not overtly attacked; by implication it is brought under scrutiny at the very least, the charge being that traditional skill-based musical activity for all too often means twelve year olds, for example, who are coping with binary mathematics, indices, equations, or concepts such as democracy, being given nothing more challenging than simple basic rhythms and melody patterns in music lessons at a level of intellectual and physical functioning more appropriate to a normal child many years younger. One of the claims for experimental musical activities is that it challenges students at an appropriate level commensurate with their stage of maturation. This merits some examination.

While it is possible to detect some common threads in both rationale and content in a number of publications on experimental music, they all tend to reflect originality in the sense that they are different in scope and content from what has been traditionally practised in schools. They also show undoubted influences of earlier work by composers such as Cage and Varèse. One of the most identifiably original is R. Murray Schafer. *The Composer in the Classroom* and *Ear Cleaning* represent a radical approach to music education, though not an entirely new one in the context of musical activities of this century. Stockhausen had said earlier than the 1960s that it was necessary to listen as never before, and a number of composers had suggested the need for developing new listening abilities to cope with their new concepts of music. However, it would be wrong to assume that Murray Schafer is as radical in content as he is in approach. He seeks to throw new light on musical tradition through his approach, as exemplified in the two works mentioned, rather than invent a new musical tradition.

Murray Schafer — *The Composer in the Classroom* and *Ear Cleaning*

The Composer in the Classroom was published in Canada in 1965 but reports some teaching carried out the previous year. The organisation and content of the short book, while owing something to Cage's methods in *Silence* (first published in 1939), owe very little to Cage's musical content. Indeed Schafer is attempting to get his students to think about traditional, historical music in new ways. The teaching process is described in detail. There are six sections, each of which contains essential points of discussion between Schafer and his students. At times it is somewhat reminiscent of the conversations Debussy invented with his "alter ego," M. Croche.

The first discussion is about musical taste, and the students, all practising musicians from various schools on a Canadian Summer Music School, are guided through a discussion on the diversity of music and taste. Next the question "What is Music?" is explored, and this involves identifying distinctions between noise and music. The importance of context is mentioned, and the class is encouraged to experiment with sound to illustrate various points of discussion. The third discussion is entitled "Descriptive Music," and the class is encouraged to improvise on their instruments. There is a description in sound of a flight of a bird played on a flute. The swooping, circling and soaring expected of a bird's movements are represented graphically as an aid. Another sound picture is created, this time of fog. One significant exchange illustrates the reluctance of trained musicians to make sounds that are comparatively arbitrary. A trumpet player, for example, would not invent a fanfare, and a teacher observing Schafer, but obviously out of touch with the discussion, calls out, "Yeoman Bold, page 5." Schafer comments, "Fortunately the trumpeter is still reluctant." Other discussions deal with textures, music, and conversation, with, finally, a composition session based on a poem by Brecht — "Mask of the Evil Demon."

Throughout, Schafer relates concepts of sound with music of any age and is not averse to referring to composers both past and present to illustrate some point. He is not overtly relating to contemporary music but is rather presenting musical traditions in contemporary manner. He also introduces graphic notations for the sounds produced where conventional notations are inadequate.

In the introduction to *Ear Cleaning* we get some idea of Schafer's personal starting point through the words of Keith Bissell:

> R. Murray Schafer is a major Canadian composer . . . a gifted teacher .
> . . whose technique in the classroom . . . is refreshingly unorthodox . . .
> flexible, socratic, and deceptively improvisatory; it invariably produces
> an enthusiastic and significant response from his students . . . He main-
> tains that ears must be cleaned as a prerequisite for all music listening
> and playing . . . the common denominator of all lessons is active student
> participation through free discussion, experimentation, improvisation
> and objective analysis of all elements of music. No conclusion is ac-
> cepted until thoroughly tested in the crucible of personal experience.

In his notes to the lectures Schafer makes some pertinent comments about music teaching in general. He writes of teachers who "play disc jockey to the great, invariably dead composers" and of his belief that one learns "practically nothing about the actual functioning of music by sitting in mute surrender before it." *Ear Cleaning* was published two years after *The Composer in the Classroom*. In this book Schafer explores similar territory but with a more overt philosophical standpoint attempted, related to the central role of expectation in our listening habits. Training students to sit in "mute surrender before" so called "great" artworks is not a part of his educative function. Instead he advocates making sounds themselves and examining the results. "One cannot always assemble a symphony orchestra in the classroom to feel the sensations," therefore the teacher should make use of whatever is available. The sounds produced may be crude, he concedes, but "they are ours," and "an actual contact with musical sounds is made." This he maintains is more vital than listening programs. He goes on to say that the student "learns something very practical about the size and shape of things musical." What he means by this can be deduced from

the "lectures" that follow his introductory notes. Each lecture is focused on a topic. The first is entitled "Noise," then come "Silence,"
"Tone," "Timbre," "Amplitude," "Melody," "Texture," etc., each dealing
with the respective aspect of sound suggested by the title.

Since the book is entitled *Ear Cleaning* it is perhaps important to be
sure what he means by this term. He explains in his introductory
notes that the primary task is to "open ears" and to "notice sounds they
have never listened to before." Furthermore, before "ear training" we
require, "ear cleaning." He likens it to a surgeon washing his hands before a delicate operation. He seems to be saying, therefore, that the
business of ear cleaning is tantamount to a surgeon washing his
hands, but is this so? Does he really mean "cleaning" in the same
sense?

Unfortunately, the term *ear cleaning* has become a slogan for some
trendy music teachers whose perceptions of its meaning have been
vague, to say the least. Schafer goes on to say that the ear is vulner-
able and cannot be closed like the eye; its only protection is psychological filtering, resulting in the ear becoming "blunted" to sound.
After this point he stops defining his technique and goes on to more
philosophical and artistic matters.

It is difficult to accept the term *ear cleaning* in the sense presented.
It is surely impossible to eradicate auditory sensations encoded in
memory in the same way that one can wash off dirt from the hands
with detergents. So he does not, or he cannot mean washing in this
sense. Elsewhere he appears to be advocating exposure rather than
limitation, so his ear cleaning technique has to do with *opening* and
with selection of auditory sensation. He advocates personal contact
with sound as the basic ingredient of music, however crude the
sound, in order that the students learn something about the "size and
shape of things musical." There is undoubtedly a similar desire expressed here to that by Stockhausen, outlined in Chapter 5. The object there was to become aware of every parameter of sound equally
and to be aware of every detail rather than "vast preordained
schemes." This was an aid to listening to new music. Schafer seems
to be saying something similar, yet with a difference. He advocates
"opening ears to all sounds so as to develop appreciation of sounds
which truly matter." The problem lies in identifying "sounds which
truly matter." What criteria are to be applied to such judgements?
Here is the place for no conclusion being accepted "until thoroughly

tested in the crucible of personal experience." It is this exploration of sound which is the innovative feature of Schafer's approach. Exploration with a purpose is being able to develop, through personal experience, critical faculties in judging the effect of sounds, first those produced by the students "exploring" sound, then those from other sources around them. After this Schafer turns to examples from the art of music. The sequence then becomes clear as movement from the generality of sound as it exists in the world around us towards the specific experience of art music, and on the way, during this process of aural education, the student develops "ear cleaning," which is to say discrimination powers based upon his or her own personal standards and background.

For example, the lecture on "Melody" starts with the generalities of frequency movement, "moving the tone to different altitudes," as he puts it. It progresses to more specific movement, illustrated graphically, and ends up with examining the pitch movement in the aria from Bach's Magnificat in D, "Deposuit Potentes," where Bach has painted the words in true baroque manner by matching the word *down* with a downward movement in pitch. The lecture on "Texture" starts with an explanation of contrapuntal structures in music, moves on to graphic representations of different textures, and ends with a mention of Tallis's 40 part motet *Spem in Alium*. Thus the sequence and focus become clear in these lectures. Schafer seeks to explain musical structure as it occurred in history from generality to specificity, from allusion to musical reality, from auditory awareness of the sensation of sound to cultured awareness of art music, and from visual understanding to auditory in some examples.

One thing can be dispelled for sure; Schafer is not preaching illiteracy or vague experiments in sound. He is proposing a structured music appreciation course that is tightly organized and designed to explain complex concepts of musical elements to a nonhomogeneous group of students, i.e. whose backgrounds are enormously varied in musical attainment and experience. Far from being exposed to charges of musical heresy, the content of *Ear Cleaning* is testimony to a desire to disseminate knowledge and experience of the elements of the art of music of all ages and styles. It is the product of a sensitive musician responding in a sensitive fashion to the problems he is confronted with in the classroom as he goes about the daily task of earning a living teaching music. The concept is unique and brilliant and intended to eradicate auditory illiteracy or bias induced by cultural conditioning. "Ear cleaning" is the term, but ear opening is the product towards a more discriminating auditory awareness.

George Self — *New Sounds in Class* (1967)

George Self describes *New Sounds in Class* as a "practical approach to the understanding and performing of contemporary music in schools." Unlike the Schafer book, this one is unashamedly propagating the use of contemporary music as an end in itself. A note at the beginning indicates that the experimental work described in the book was carried out in part in a school and a college for educating teachers. The foreword refers to hostility towards modern music and suggests evidence of some change in this respect enabling such music to become somewhat more acceptable. One factor suggested is an increase in accessibility through recordings and performances. Moreover, Self comments upon developments at the tertiary level of education in music:

> More teachers, who have absorbed at Universities and Training Colleges some of the modern compositional techniques, and their classroom applications should feel less isolated from the contemporary musical scene, and from general educational thought than their predecessors.

He sees his book as a first experience of modern music:

> The suggestions and material in this book make a useful starting point. Further work may be done with published compositions, with pupil's own compositions, and one hopes, with those of the teacher.

In the introduction Self explains that

> in almost all so-called modern educational music, the pupils play or sing particular sounds in specified rhythms at tempi decided on by the composer. In this way skill at reading is systematically developed.

He goes on to point out that

> meanwhile, in the plastic arts and sciences, pupils are learning to recognize and use language of their own time. Musical education seems to lag far behind, and the aim of this book is to form a link between contemporary music and instrumental work in the classroom. It is not intended to provide an alternative to existing methods . . . but to be complementary.

Having stated the objective as simply one concerned with introducing contemporary music to the classroom, Self briefly explains some of the new trends, pointing out the rate of change in this century, and mentioning some composers.

Of particular importance to Self is the need for new notations for the new sounds he proposes. However, he does use conventional notation as far as possible so that "the work may be integrated with existing school material" (p. 10). He explains the use of the new notations he employs by describing new ways of using elements such as pitch, time, and timbre. There will be no regular beat, for example, in the early exercises, and the diatonic scale plays "little part in today's music," so he begins with "all sounds available." He goes on to state that "to limit the sounds to those of the major scale is to train for the past and for pop music." He advocates the use of any instrument available in this work in class.

The new notations Self employs are simple and easy to understand. Basic movements in parameters of sound are designated in logical fashion. A short sound is symbolised by a dot, whereas a long sound is a long shape. The pieces that form the basis of the work range from very short items, where everyone plays the same single short sounds, manipulating dynamics between loud (f) and soft (p), to highly complex structures where a number of parameters are being manipulated. At this point there are combinations of short and long, fast and slow, precise musical rhythms and single sounds that just fade naturally, together with many different instrumental timbres. The time element in all the pieces is controlled by means of time frames. These are merely numbered so that at whatever point in time the conductor feels it appropriate he can signal the change. For Piece no. 1, for example, Self explains (see p. 17): "The speed at which the piece is taken will depend on the ability of the pupils, acoustics of the room and the effect desired by the conductor." Self's pieces are really varying manipulations of different parameters of sound, ranging from extremely simple, as in Piece no. 1, to comparatively complex as in the final Piece 22, entitled "Variations." It is a first book of its kind, and its aims are simply to introduce the use of contemporary music. There is no attempt at relating logically any of the events in contemporary music to the choice of activity in his pieces. He feels that the first stage in the use of contemporary music should be in manipulating basic parameters of sound and in developing an ability to perform these basic manipulations from a mixture of invented and conventional notations. Although lamenting the way music education lags behind the plastic arts in educational practise there is no cogent argument presented other than to state that music should be as contemporary as other school subjects, which in itself is not a cogent argument.

John Paynter and Peter Aston — *Sound and Silence* (1970)

Perhaps the most substantial publication of the period is *Sound and Silence* by John Paynter and Peter Aston (1970). Its subtitle, "Classroom Projects in Creative Music," gives the reader the substance of the book. There is a fairly lengthy introduction followed by thirty-six projects that explore many different facets of music and other arts in various relationships. The focus is on contemporary music throughout, and something of the rationale is indicated by the quotation of Luciano Berio preceding the contents page: "Through music today it is possible to be aware of reality in a very important way." In the general introduction, subtitled "Music in a Liberal Education," the development of awareness through music and the arts is the theme. Awareness through intuitive acts, in this case music making, is suggested. Examples are cited of the authors' experiences: a boy aged six pretending to be a wolf and making wolf noises, a group of teenagers making intuitive harmony round a campfire, and two students making intuitive music in an unconventional fashion and going through the process of "refining and developing" ideas. The preface contains a list of schools with dates, the earliest being 1963, indicating extensive experimental work with children and older students.

A notion of music in a liberal education is expounded throughout the introduction. First, the question is asked, "Why do we teach music anyway?" Partly in answer is the following:

> Apart from those of us who are concerned solely with certain clearly defined skills such as techniques of playing instruments, the work of most teachers in schools is essentially a contribution to the general education of children . . . Even if a teacher finds himself working in a school as "the music specialist" . . . he must not let this cause him to forget his first duty: the education of the whole person. He makes a contribution to this "total education" through the medium of his own subject. (p. 2)

Earlier, the authors draw attention to the distinction between general and specialist forms of education, as applied to music. They go on to explicate their notions of a liberal education, which, by implication, is general and for everyone, unlike specialist education.

> The liberal education we wish for our children implies a breadth of understanding and experience that will be possible only when we consciously make efforts to remove the boundaries between subjects . . . it is as a creative art that music is beginning to play an increasingly important role in education . . . it is language and, as a vehicle for expression, it is available in some degree to everyone. (p. 3)

A liberal education requires the "removal of subject barriers." The authors point out that no subject can "live if left in a box by itself . . . it is part of the wide field of human experience and needs to be understood in that context first" (p. 2). The rationale for integration of subjects is revealed, namely that "all knowledge comes from experience of life." It is not a very convincing one.

Following this point Paynter and Aston go on to the role of creativity and the arts as a response to life. They seem to be saying that children should be encouraged to develop the ability to see the world as intensely as do artists and to learn to express themselves in many different media.

> But the artist does more than a make a record: he projects feelings into his materials — paint, wood, stone, words, movement, sound, or whatever — until the materials become like the reality of his imagination. (p. 3)

They go on to say that we see and hear such work through the eyes and ears of the artist. Thus we see the world differently than we normally do by "looking" at it through the work of the artist. The authors mention the work of Marion Richardson and Herbert Read in showing how art in education should begin with what "the individual has to say."

Further, the work of others is cited to support the notion of children expressing themselves — their views of the world and the things they care deeply about — through various media including words, visual organizations of materials, movement, drama, and of course, music. Moreover, the accessibility of contemporary styles and materials and their relevance as a living language are cited as vital factors in their use in education.

> On the walls of our Primary School classrooms we can see paintings
> which reflect the experiments of painters like Jackson Pollock, Paul
> Klee, and Ben Nicholson . . . David Holbrook suggests literature the
> children would appreciate . . . works by Joyce, Lawrence etc . . . The
> boys and girls we teach rarely seem to find difficulty with the language
> of contemporary art. Young people today have an outlook which chimes
> in with the liberalism of the twentieth-century directions . . . Music can
> be approached in the same way. (p. 6)

The final part of the introduction explicates the ethos of the projects.
Music can only be understood by exploring the medium and its potential. This can be achieved through creative music, which is a way
of saying things that are personal to the individual.

> It also implies freedom to explore chosen materials . . . [the teacher's]
> role is to set off trains of thought and help the pupil develop his own
> critical powers and perceptions . . . the processes . . . are selection and
> rejection, evaluation and confirming the material . . . essentially an ex-
> perimental situation. (p. 7)

The book "sets out to provide suggestions for creative experiment in
music" (p. 7) and emphasizes exploration rather than implanting
concepts and facts. The authors finish the introduction with the
statement, "The true rudiments of music are to be found in an exploration of its materials — sound and silence" (p. 8).

Although apparently radical in the context of music education in
the classroom and seemingly supported by then current notions of
what education was supposed to be all about, *Sound and Silence* did
not altogether address the problems of classroom music successfully.
Conceived in the late 1960s, it is redolent of notions of liberal, child-
centred educational theory, and although Paynter and Aston attempt to contribute far more to the debate concerning education as a
whole and music's place in it, the results are far from satisfactory.
One is not sure whether there is reference to R.S. Peters's notion of a
liberal education, or to Dewey's. In any case the notion is far more
complex with either than is explicated by Paynter and Aston. They
touch upon distinctions between specialist and generalist educational content, indicating that there is a distinction, but they do not
explain whether they feel the distinction is in content or in methods,
or even in both. The content of the projects is an uneasy mixture of
the traditional and avant-garde. There is no convincing argument
about why one or either is necessary. There is an overt assumption

that involvement can be most easily achieved through new music, yet there are many projects involving complex concepts from historical music. It is as though they wish to satisfy both the traditionalist and the experimentalist in themselves. This is, of course, a perfectly reasonable standpoint. Many musicans feel they can tolerate experimental music provided they can relate it to or detect immediate development from traditional music, by which is usually meant the well-known concert repertoire of eighteenth and nineteenth century music.

Such attitudes reflect caution rather than understanding of the contemporary artist. It is on the educational ground that the authors attempt to build their justification for the content and methodology of the projects that there is identifiable weakness in their case. The projects do not constitute either a complete musical education or an introduction to one, and neither do the authors attempt such things. Yet what is the purpose of the book if not one or the other? Development of awareness is such a vague concept that it is not even necessary to ask development and awareness of what precisely? The quotation from Berio poses more questions than it answers: for example, what is reality? What is a "very important way"? Such a statement as that of Berio might well be appropriate to the artistic activity of a practising composer, but what relevance has it to a teacher and his students in the classroom? This is not fully addressed, since there can only be relevance to the activities of an artist, and the authors are likening children to artists in the projects and providing situations where they can act as such. One problem with this is that there is a strong body of opinion that supports entirely different, even opposite methodologies: Children cannot act like practitioners of any description until they have acquired knowledge and skill. However interesting and exciting the projects appear, they can have no adequate validity until this problem is resolved.

The Manhattanville Music Curriculum Program

During the mid-1960s in the United States a group of musicians and music educators around New York City were involved together in what became known as the Manhattanville Music Curriculum Program (MMCP). Americole Biasini, Lenore Pogonowski, and Ronald Thomas wrote the latest two publications on the project.

These are entitled *MMCP Interaction — Early Childhood Music Curriculum* and *MMCP Synthesis* and were published in 1979. Earlier publications had disseminated information across the United States, and there was extensive involvement of many schools, individuals, and school boards, as well as other bodies. The MMCP is not so much a complete curriculum as an approach. The emphasis is upon exploring and experiencing rather than implanting of fact and knowledge, and there is extensive explanation of the approach and its philosophical bases. Although published in 1979, it is dealt with now, apparently out of sequence, because the content relates to earlier publications and classroom experiments. "Interaction," for early childhood music education, is described in the preface as

> a comprehensive early childhood music learning plan . . . a basic experience in musicianship for children of the preprimary and primary grades . . . is process-oriented, the experience of personal involvement is the goal . . . the only concern for sequence . . . is found in the processes of exploration called the Developmental Processes of Musical Exploration (DPME).

The preface further states that "the learning program described can be successfully implemented by the classroom teacher with consultative assistance from a musical specialist." At this level of education it is necessary to know this since so many schemes for teaching music require specialist knowledge from the teacher. A precise focus is indicated throughout: "With the classroom teacher guiding and initiating musical activities the children can be offered a much broader range of musical involvement." Finally, the preface explains:

> Interaction is not an exclusive learning plan . . . [it] deals with creative operations, with discovery, personal exploration and judgement. Whilst such activities should be the core of the child's musical involvment, many other types of experience may be made available . . . singing, listening, dancing, painting, and theatre are strongly encouraged.

The process of a musical education is dealt with. There is a clear rejection of rote learning and teacher-direction and highly circumscribed task-oriented educational methodology. Instead there is a compelling and detailed account of the nature of the child's experiences and the learning operations that need planning in some detail. Concerning these matters an important point is made in the introduction:

> . . . the understanding of music is entirely different from the develop-
> ment of proficiencies in the mechanics of musical symbols and systems.
> It is also different from learning the very precise kinesthetic skills related
> to musical performances. (p. ix)

One has to do with internalizing experience, with "intrinsic feeling and personal values and attitudes," whereas the other has to do with "prescribed acts and tutored proficiencies" (p. ix). The introduction goes on to elucidate in a very positive manner a wholly child-centered approach to education.

The child's already acquired methods of organizing experience are emphasized, and the school is cast in the role of an unfeeling imposer of alien (to the child) facts, methodologies, and criteria, if the approach to teaching does not account sufficiently for the child's own experiences. Reference is also made to the differences between the child's perception of the world (music) and the adult's and to the significance of music as not being something special to school but occurring all around the child in daily life.

> [The child] is already full of musical ideas, curiosity and things to say in
> sound . . . he needs outlets for his musicianship far more than input . . .
> he thinks in a musical way and has a sense of aural logic long before he
> comes to school . . . has seemingly endless imagination and is self-
> motivated when opportunities for self-expression and exploration are
> made available to him. (p. xii)

The "Rationale" contains a number of compelling arguments in favour of the general approach to MMCP. Creativity is a prominent feature of the argument. Unfortunately, like so many arguments that use creativity as a buttress, the intended meaning of the word is hazy. In this case it could be interchangeable with curiosity. There is reference to "man's propensity to probe the unknown, to experience the world imaginatively and to form impressions from his contact with the elements in his environment" (p. 1) and later to the removal of "inhibiting" factors in the teaching situation. Creativity is confused with a process of exploration and the use of this process as a tool with which to generate interest in music. If one can say that creativity means the process and product of a Mozart conceiving and writing and completing his Symphony in G Minor no. 40 then it is something more than mere curiosity and exploration of sound. This is a much more complex argument than there is space for at this point. The important thing is that although the authors use the word *creativity,* they do go on to specify in some detail what they conceive the process and its relevance to a number of aspects to be. For instance they advocate "free exploration of sounds in the classroom," and the inevitable noise is called "creative fall-out" (p. 1). This is not necessarily so far removed from the kind of situation one imagines composers such as J.S. Bach, Beethoven, and Chopin to be involved in as they improvised, that is tried out their musical ideas in sound, before committing themselves to paper. There must have been a good deal of "creative fall-out" in the process. Indeed Beethoven's notebooks would tend to confirm this. If this is creativity then it clearly has validity not only in the world of musical artists but possibly in education, if one wants to provide situations for children that resemble those of the artist in acts of "creating" music. Unanswered educational problems are raised, however, when we read: "Today it is widely recognized that children have a remarkable capacity for teaching themselves, for assimilating and organizing that information which is in some way useful to them" (p. 2).

It is obvious to anyone who has taught in institutions that this does not happen in the institutional classroom. Apart from the difficulty of knowing what is useful to children, there is an apparent confusion, for an earlier statement advocated guidance by the teacher in explorations and discoveries. However impressed one might be by the enthusiasm and fluency of the argument, there is thus a lack of clarity concerning both methodology and content implicit in such comments even though the schema specifies free and ordered activities separately. Other comments such as "The condition of understanding implies self-discerned meaning, personal judgement, and a relevance to one's own life style . . . understanding suggests intrinsic feeling and personal values and attitudes" (p. ix) raise many questions about the aims and purposes of education. Can it really be held that education has no more to offer than merely allowing the right conditions to exist for the child to explore and develop his own values and standards? Is there no place for educating him in the values of a society, culture, or nation? Is he to be allowed to grow up with a haphazardly organized experience of such things? The authors are clearly relating to the early stages of music education and attempting to elucidate their theoretical standpoint concerning education at this early stage, and with sympathy one can understand. However, a hard-line traditionalist supporting direction and implanting would not be convinced by such arguments, and neither would someone searching for a valid definition of the processes and nature of education, not to mention its product.

The message is clear. The child is not seen as a spectator in music but an active participant, and lack of traditional performance skills should not in any way be an inhibiting factor in the exploring processes referred to. Moreover, the child must not be presented with music as though it were a static art form. It is seen as constantly growing and expanding, changing and shifting in emphasis.

Particularly interesting is the passage on symbolism in music (p. 6). Here is emphasized the importance of individual symbolism and the difficulty inherent in perceiving another's symbolic meaning. Since symbols are a product of experience, they are unique in both meaning and function to the experience and the individual who "owns it," so to speak.

> Symbolic codes grow out of a felt need to objectify experience. Other people's symbols do not necessarily contain meaning for the child, unless he understands the process through which they were generated. (p. 6)

Implicit in this argument are some psychological reasons for the processes advocated in *Interaction* and evidence is presented from a number of sources in support; for example:

> Jean Piaget has said, "Even in order to understand we have to invent, or that is, to reinvent, because we can't start from the beginning again. But I would say that anything is only understood to the extent that it is reinvented." (p. 6)

The book is a very detailed explanation of a methodology for a musical education for the younger child, and even though some of the terminology invites questions concerning clarity, the detail of explanation and sequence presents a clear model for the teacher to follow. It is not a set of classroom recipes or even projects intended to explore different facets of music of some kind. It is essentially an explanation of an approach to teaching music, starting with an exploration of sound itself, within the defined capabilities of the child. Knowledge of psychological processes inherent in children's responses to their environment is applied, and an appropriate sequence of activities, both free and guided, is suggested. The planned detail is meticulous in presentation, and the information presented is exhaustive. From the "Introduction" and "Rationale," through "The Shape of the Curriculum," an overview of the total process, a description of the process — "Curriculum Operations" — and to samples of "Operational Plans" each with its own fully explained sequence of activities and educational criteria, to the "Glossary of Terms," a list of "Unconventional Sound Sources" and a "Discography," there is evident a meticulous level of detailed planning that presents to the teacher strategies and sequenced learning schemes designed to provide increasingly more atomistic and critical involvement in organizing sound.

Part IV, "Operational Plans," shows five phases of sequential activity designed to involve "children in the Development Phases of Musical Exploration" (p. 39). Each phase shows "a Sample Encounter, Principal Ideas, Objectives for Pupils, Procedures for Teachers, and Evaluative Criteria" (p. 39). There is a fully explicit description and definition of DPME in Part II ("The Shape of the Curriculum"), and each phase of DPME thus described is treated to the same sequence of activities explained under "Operational Plans." For example, phase 1 of DPME ("Free Exploration") is organized sequentially as follows:

1. Sample Encounters — with detailed procedures for exploring sound with different types of paper materials.
2. Principal Ideas — the stage of exploring sound and materials that can produce them, with more precise identification and classification.
3. Objectives — under subheadings of skill, cognitive and attitudinal objectives designed to expand awareness through comparison, similarities, and more guided critical awareness.
4. Procedures — involving suggestions for the teacher in the implementation of the phases.
5. Evaluations — a series of questions, the answers to which indicate reasons for success or failure for the teacher.

Each of the following four phases of DPME is organized similarly with the activity becoming more specifically focused. The sound-producing capabilities of various types of paper serve as a model to illustrate classroom activities. There seems to be some merit in this from a strictly utilitarian point of view in that such materials are readily available anywhere and cost nothing. However, under phase 1 of DPME ("Free Exploration") the following instructions indicate flexibility for the imaginative teacher.

> Sounds can be produced by materials not commonly considered as musical sound sources such as a wide variety of paper products. There are many ways to produce sounds. There is an infinite variety of sounds. All sounds are different: sometimes the differences are big, sometimes little. (p. 45)

Following the fully detailed series of phases using paper materials to produce sounds for exploration, manipulation, and organization, there are two "Alternate Series" (p. 93). The first is subtitled "Metal Encounters" and suggests the use of metal instead of paper, and the second suggests the use of the voice.

Thus by the end of *Interaction* the children will have experienced a wide range of concepts in sound and some specific musical ones at the discretion of the teacher. This type of foundation is seen as a more suitable basis upon which to build specific musical concept development later through the schemes of MMCP "Synthesis." This book is even more deliberately radical than "Interaction" because it focuses more directly upon musical practises, suggests some radical standpoints as well as clear educational ideology. Hints of both are found in the preface. This comprises a series of short statements about music and education, some specifically musical, some educational, and some a mixture of both. For example, "music is either pre- or post-Webern," a statement that is both provocative and illuminating depending upon one's depth of interest and education in twentieth century music, and "Bruner could have written 'The Processes of Education' just about music" together indicate an involvement with the contemporary in both musical and educational thought that challenges the traditional in both.

There follows a lengthy statement about the nature of the general approach of MMCP, which is organized under various headings and subheadings in an attempt to display the arguments with clarity. Preceding the introduction is a short quotation that comments on how in traditional educational practises the teaching method has taken the place of the discipline it is supposed to elucidate, and the result is that children learn skills rather than the subject matter. Here is the heart of the whole argument supporting MMCP. The approach advocates development of understanding of music, not mere skill acquisition, and there is a most detailed and comprehensive statement in support that covers many different facets of discussion.

The introduction deals with the issue of relevance, in particular the observed rejection of school music by students over the age of about twelve years. Cited as reasons are lack of awareness of the need to account for the arrival of the Piagetian stage of formal operations, relevance to the individual's needs in music, to his social environment, and to contemporary music: "Music in school is a re-creation of historical monuments" sums up the last point.

The "Rationale" deals with the nature of music, a formidable topic indeed, but one that is dealt with in simple fashion. Three characteristics of music are identified that can be of use in the educational context. First, music is an "agent for the projection and clarification of thought" (p. 5). The assumption is that the musician should not be dependent upon verbal or written explanations of music "in order to make judgements or respond to musical stimuli" (p. 6). Some doubt must exist over whether such is true. Apart from the problem of the artist being asked to explain his art even to a friendly observer there is surely a need to convey something of the precise nature of an artistic concept, and this can only be done using words. Admittedly a verbal explanation cannot adequately account for a musical experience, but it can help to illuminate it and provide a bit more insight into the artist's use of materials. This must be of some help to those willing to listen and learn. In any case musical history is full of examples of misunderstood composers whose works become known, liked, and understood through means of verbal comment. As far as MMCP is concerned the point is clear: Musical actions speak louder than words. The second characteristic is that musicians "in the creative aspects of involvement, are concerned with the musical thought of our time" (p. 6). Since MMCP is conceived as being pupils' creative involvement with music, this is an important point. Historical music is not precluded as a source of appreciation, but it is as a source of creative actions, the reason being that "a musician is a contributor to the continual development of musical thought and practice . . . music is a continuing art and not a static or completed set of occurrences" (p. 6). The meaning of creativity is confined by this statement to involvement with the new. It appears that in such a definition it is not possible to be creative with the established unless one is developing new from old. The practises exemplified in MMCP would tend to support this definition of creativity.

The third characteristic concerns the need for individual creative activity, and this is related to the issue of relevance to the individual. There follows the identification of various objectives — cognitive, attitudinal, skill, and aesthetic — as well as evaluation processes. Great emphasis is placed upon clarity of presentation to the student both of the task and of expectation concerning results. The section headed "Principles of MMCP Curriculum" focuses with greater clarity on the educational applications of the approach. The applications are always presented as subservient to answers to much more fundamental questions about the nature of music, the purpose of education, and the starting point of the pupil. The following illustrates the point: "In the development of the MMCP curriculum, the first and most significant step was the clarification of a basic position on the nature of music" (p. 15). From this basic position arose the behaviours that form the content of the MMCp. Similarly a basic position regarding the nature of the student was reached, and this was obtained from the works of "Bruner, Holt, Piaget, Parnes and others" (p. 15). Thus the whole approach is explicated in terms that relate to underling beliefs and principles. For example, the focus in learning activities is as follows:

> Inductive, deductive and intuitive reasoning, the discovery oriented strategies and the obvious concern for the development of analytical, judicial and creative thinking were all consistent with decisions regarding the nature of the learner. (p. 15)

Clearly a most overt, child-centred strategy is at the heart of the educative process of MMCP. Discovery rather than instruction, self-directed learning situations rather than teacher-directed activities are the focus. Discovery means, in MMCP terms, "first hand experience, intrinsic involvement" (p. 16). Discovery is further defined as "creative discovery," and the reader is warned that it should not be misinterpreted to include "clever observation." By this is meant "recognition of factors which, while they may evoke a personal response, are basically external" (p. 16). The argument is detailed and intricate but not entirely convincing, for how can one discover entirely from personal experience the intrinsic values of a historical work of art? If one cannot, then where in the scheme of things does an education for appreciation of such come? In the detailed content of cycles and strategies it appears that one should explore a particular aspect of musical language and then listen to recordings of works that exemplify it. This comes after extensive examination of the works completed by students in the exploring process, which is in fact a problem-solving situation in the manner expounded by Bruner. Thus concept understanding is the primary goal of the curriculum to be achieved through "discovery" rather than through mere "observation."

A most important distinction is made concerning two basic types of concept. Inherent concepts are described as those pertaining primarily "to the basic characteristics of the materials of music" (p. 17). On the other hand idiomatic concepts are those

> which deal with period practices, with the organizational schemes which have been devised by composers at one time or another in the history of music. Melody, in the style of eighteenth century practice, the IV, V, I cadence, rock rhythms, etc. are all very valid musical ideas but must be classified as idiomatic concepts. (p. 17).

The distinction is clear, but the reasoning does not take into account that inherent concepts may also be idiomatic concepts. Moreover, with the discovery methods advocated it is not at all inconceivable that students may be working with what to them are inherent concepts but to a knowledgeable musician are idiomatic. Of some importance is the distinction between these two for the working of the curriculum, for the student should not have "idiomatic concepts represented as enduring qualities" (p. 17). This presupposes that inherent concepts are somehow different from idiomatic ones. The possibility is ignored that the students' work may be intended to be inherent but may well be idiomatic.

The question arises whether it is possible to make this kind of distinction. The objective is clear: it is to avoid simplistic training in historical practises. It is anathema to the MMCP philosophy that music education should be concerned with learning about musical history, great composers, and great pieces of music. The development of musical concepts through personal involvement is the aim even though this may include listening to historical music.

Perhaps a clearer understanding of the aims can be achieved from the following: "Music of our time is the most logical place to begin music study. It is relevant artistically and educationally" (p. 20). This relates to the notion that the "music of today, the contemporary art, is the product of centuries of growth and many thousands of compositions . . . a creative extension of earlier music thought" (p. 19). The underlying assumption is that today's music is a kind of culmination of what has gone before; while not overtly stated, it is also implied that a study of contemporary music in the manner suggested in the curriculum will also acquaint the student with principles that are applicable to all music both past and present.

This is a most difficult claim to accept. Music is not an art form that is linear in progression but one that tends to be subject to changing fashions, different cultural milieux, and different criteria of expressive content and purpose. One cannot have it both ways: music cannot be relevant to today, the "here and now" and also be the "sum of its history." It is difficult to see how some electronic music of the avant-garde can be regarded as a synthesis of some of the past in the way Brahms' fourth Symphony might be, for example. While the MMCP might call educationally for an "artistic frame of reference . . . grounded on the here and now (and) the meaning of music (should) be viewed through a perspective which is compatible with the viability of the art" (p. 20), it is a much more difficult thing to justify in artistic as well as educational terms. Educationally the justification is in the following:

> The emphasis of music education should . . . be on the development of sensitive people who have the breadth of insight and skill proficiency to use music for its intrinsic meaning and value to them.

The detail of *MMCP Synthesis* is remarkably clear in setting out its spiral curriculum, and the sequence of activities is exciting and relevant to both the student and educational aims concerned with child-centred discovery methods of dealing with knowledge. The musical arguments are not so clear or so watertight. While it may be educationally valid to concentrate on the contemporary in view of the discovery method described, this kind of approach may be regarded by some as too extreme or biased, in which case the MMCP can be regarded as questionable in its content and aims. However the actual content as described in the cycles is not so extreme as it may appear. There is evidence of development through personal discovery, which would probably please all but the most hardened teacher-director of learning. A brief look at one aspect — timbre — through several cycles can illustrate well the kind of sequence in MMCP. In cycle 2 timbre has to do with contrast and tasks are set on this; in cycle 5 it has to do with combined sounds; by cycle 10 it is concerned with polyphony and harmony to achieve homogeneity or contrast as necessary.

The sequence of activity suggested outlines a gradually more complex type of sound. Instead of the simple contrasts of cycle 1, in the later cycles there is a need to listen for contrast with a keener sense of aural discrimination. Timbre is used in a general sense to indicate differences in complexity of sounds rather than a more atomistic approach investigating the nature of timbre and the composition of sound itself. This approach demands that students develop a sophisticated understanding of purely musical notions such as polyphony and harmony.

In the case of pitch cycle 1 is concerned with relative highness and lowness. A cymbal sounds low in comparison with a triangle but high compared with a drum. By cycle 4 pitch involves pentatonic groups of notes and the use of treble clef. By cycle 7 polyphony is explored by setting two or more different melodies together, and suggested listening includes a Bach concerto. In cycle 10 harmony is introduced simply as the combination of notes simultaneously. There is no attempt to identify tonal harmony or any kind of harmonic sequence. Listening examples include Webern's *Six Pieces for Orchestra* and Elliot Carter's *Woodwind Quintet*. Further cycles introduce triads (cycle 12), quartals, or chords built on fourths instead of thirds, (cycle 14), and clusters (cycle 16). Listening for each of these cycles involves a wide range of twentieth century music: cycle 12 lists Albert Roussel's *Trio for Flute, Viola and Cello* for example, and it is suggested that in later cycles the student should be able to listen to longer pieces of five to ten minutes' duration.

The same or similar sequence of activities is outlined under the three other elements of music: rhythm, form, and dynamics. In each there is a gradual increase in complexity of materials suggested. Thus the program is unfolded through the 16 cycles, but they are meant to indicate the general approach rather than to constitute an actual program. In the same way that MMCP advocates child-centred learning so the implication is that the teacher should plan his/her own program using the examples given as a guide and the lengthy explanatory chapters preceding as the philosophical under-pinning.

The layout of this publication is meticulous in all respects, and the teacher is shown a level of detailed planning and organization that is nothing but impressive. On this the MMCP is faultless. It is, however, on a deeper level that questions arise. For example, sequence indicates some kind of development from one level to another, and it is difficult to see precisely how the use of clusters under the heading "Pitch" constitutes a development from the use of chords built in fourths. In this way the spiral concept of development is perhaps a little shaky in its claims as exemplified in these examples. A much more fundamental question arises concerning planning in musical education. Dealt with in this manner can there be such a thing as sequence implying higher and higher levels of conceptual understanding? Is it a matter of merely being different or of being on a higher conceptual plane? When Beethoven, for example, introduced a greater emphasis on contrapuntal as opposed to harmonic content in his compositions was he moving to a higher plane of thought or merely a different one? In this case also there was an increase in complexity implicit, but does such an increase automatically mean higher conceptually? It is difficult to see how it can be higher in terms of concepts. His Fifth Symphony is surely as difficult conceptually as any of his late quartets in terms of formal structure! In the same way the cycles of *MMCP Synthesis* suggest different configurations of materials, not successively higher levels of concept formation.

It is perhaps significant that Paynter and Aston did not attempt to indicate sequence, merely to suggest a number of projects of varying complexity in the use of materials. They do not touch the subject of sequence to any degree in their philosophical arguments, but neither do they attempt the level of sophisticated planning achieved in MMCP. Certainly an increase in complexity is one way to suggest a progression, but is it the right kind of progression in activities of this type? In the art of music an apparently simple melody of Mozart can be a much more difficult object conceptually than a very complex melodic configuration by Schoenberg or Messiaen. Each will be used in a different manner, and it is this which gives it its level of conceptual difficulty. The matter of context is of great importance in music. If there is weakness in MMCP it is probably here. The concentration on contemporary music, using various definitions and classifications of materials by such figures as Persichetti (1961) in his book on twentieth century harmony, tends to ignore this matter of context and therefore style. It is difficult to see how the sequence of activity from students' improvisations to listening would not be equally effective using historical music, despite the distinction made between idiomatic and inherent referred to above. It is also difficult to accept that a more complete musical understanding would not be developed using historical material as well as contemporary, or that a more comprehensive use of contemporary material than is contained in MMCP would not be more advantagous. This is not precluded by the authors, since the general approach is not meant to be exclusive in content, merely prescriptive in philosophical approach to music education.

Brian Dennis — *Experimental Music in Schools* (1970)

The above publications illustrate what might be called the first wave of materials reflecting the use of experimental music in the classroom. There followed during the 1970s many more books, mostly short and concerned with one or more aspects of contemporary musical practises. Following on from George Self's *New Sounds in Class* Brian Dennis produced a short book entitled *Experimental Music in Schools — Towards a New World of Sound* (1970). This is in the same category as the Self book, since it is meant to introduce aspects of contemporary music to the classroom:

> The health of an art is in danger if those who teach it fall too far behind those who practise it. This book is written to help teachers who would like to introduce truly modern music to their classes. (p. 1)

There follows a short account of contemporary music, after which Dennis states:

> This is only one view of the development of twentieth-century music. Other accounts may be no less valid, but tend to ignore what to my mind has been the most significant aspect of twentieth-century music. This aspect is colour: the imaginative use of pure sound qualities, together with more complex manifestations of overall textures and sound patterning. (p. 2)

Later there is overt recognition of the influence of John Cage and his theory of indeterminacy, which is seen as representative of the "more practical alternatives . . . to the complex serial and schematic constructionalism of Boulez and Stockhausen, without evading the aesthetic implications of the music of such composers" (p. 2). It is certainly open to debate whether or not indeterminacy can do anything but evade such implications, and it is perhaps a pity that Dennis does not elaborate.

The imaginative use of "pure sound qualities" and the free processes advocated by Cage and his associates reflect one aspect of the thinking behind the schemes in the book. Listed under seven headings are the "underlying intentions of the various methods." These range from the use of notation, more radical leading to conventional, through listening, improvising, "creative activities," experimenting with sound, and the value of the pupils' own judgements in assessing values. The dissatisfaction with school music lessons is mentioned, which comprised "enforced listening periods" and "the learning of traditional notation," tending to "add up to a feeling of gloom." Instead he advocates "a feeling of lively experiment and corporate activity for all pupils involved" (p. 4).

Each chapter deals with a particular aspect. Chapter 1 is entitled "Sound out of Silence" and concerns the sound around us. The second chapter — "Improvisation" — has a number of schemes for activities, mostly using numbers as a basis for action. There follows a "short inventory of instruments." In "Pieces for the Classroom" various types of simple notations are employed, some taken directly from George Self and acknowledged as such. Chapter 4 — "Simple Creative Work" — continues with various schemes for action involving both the use of numbers and other, more graphic symbols for activities in sound. The use of some form of notation is advocated, and a scheme for improvisation is suggested. Finally there is a chapter on electronic music in the classroom, which is concerned with simple techniques using a tape recorder.

The book is a reflection of the author's own experiences teaching in a London secondary school and contains a wide variety of activities in some ways reflecting a similar range of compositional techniques to those of Paynter and Aston, particularly in the use of numbers and various graphic symbols. The shortness of the book and the relatively accessible manner of presentation for busy classroom teachers make it a handy guide for activities concerning modern music in the classroom. There is no pretension to being any more than an illustration of how certain aspects of contemporary music may be used in schools.

Robert Walker — *Sound Projects* (1976)

Another short book is *Sound Projects* by Robert Walker. The book does not state overtly that its intention is to introduce contemporary musician to the classroom. Rather it suggests that the use of schemes, or projects, while owing a great deal to contemporary musical practises, might be the only viable music education that can be offered in a classroom.

> Music in the classroom poses severe problems, chiefly to do with literacy and technique. It takes years of constant and regular musical training to master even the basic skills of reading and performing music. What can the class teacher hope to achieve in half an hour a week? (p. v)

This poses the much more fundamental question of purpose and scope of music education in a general context. Because teachers are comfortable with traditional methods in developing literacy, largely because they know little else, it is no justification for condoning low technical standards that might be achieved in such activities in the classroom. It is extremely doubtful that high technical standards can be achieved in traditional music making in a general class music lesson, as anyone who has tried it for any length of time can testify. On the other hand, through activity involving improvisation and composition based on the unorthodox techniques of this century, comparatively higher standards of aesthetic achievement can be reached. Both the process and the product are mentioned, which implies philosophical issues concerning educational purposes, though this is not explored.

Simple instructions for the teacher in selecting the instruments, working the schemes, and organizing the activities in the classroom precede details of the actual projects. There are twenty-eight projects listed under headings as follows: shapes in sound, exploring sounds, pictures in sounds, stories in sound, and abstract pieces. The last heading includes projects using numbers, improvisations employing simple patterns, and the use of various graphic notations requiring free interpretation. No particular theoretical standpoint is presented that attempts to relate the projects to actual schools or styles of twentieth century composition, but the projects are all extremely workable in the classroom where they had their genesis. This is, perhaps, an important point. *Experimental Music in Schools* is as much a didactic work as an educational tool. A particular theory concerning an aspect of modern music is suggested, and this aspect is the basis of the schemes presented. Similarly in the George Self book the simple use of graphic notations as a basis for action tends to have the same kind of didactic effect: the propogation of a particular viewpoint. By contrast, *Sound Projects* is much more an uncomplicated set of projects for making music in the classroom tied to no particular theory of modern composition by loosely borrowing ideas from many sources. This contrast poses many educational questions concerning content in the use of contemporary music in the classroom, which are as worthy of attention as those concerning the use of traditional, historical music in schools. The contrast suggested is that contemporary music needs no apology, no aesthetic justification, no particular theory to support its use in classrooms. It has at least as much right to be there as has historical music.

Gertrud Meyer-Denkmann — *Experiments in Sound* (1977)

From Cologne, Gertrud Meyer—Denkmann produced a short book on the use of sound in music education, which in its English version is entitled *Experiments in Sound* (adapted for use in English schools by Elizabeth and John Paynter). The subtitle is "New Directions in Musical Education for Young Children," and this sets the tone of the book. In the introduction the author states:

> Too much emphasis on singing and on musical games can mean that the child's learning is impeded. To offer him only an educational experience which is labelled "suitable for children" underestimates his aptitude. (p. 1)

She further states that

> there is a widespread myth that children can only "understand" music if they have been given theoretical grounding. Hans-Peter Reincecke, a specialist in the psychology of music, points out that, in music, various levels of meaning can be identified, of which those that are non-verbal, emotional or sensuous are immediately understood. (p. 1)

The idea of sequence learning is thus exploded by such notions, particularly if one is referring to children "listening to difficult works" (p. 1). The belief is that they are perfectly capable of perceiving the dimensions of sound that constitute such musical statements. Thus the argument is simply that the nature of a child's perception of the world around can be cited as an educational and musical reason for experimenting with sound in the early stages of education. Creativity is defined in terms of its recognisable characteristics:

> This means encouraging the child to discover sound as "raw materials." Let the child make sounds, listen to them critically and use his inventive intelligence to produce different "gestures," figures, and structures of sound. (p. 2).

The use of various instruments and sound-producing agencies is recommended, including experimenting with the Orff instruments found in most schools, the piano and various tools, utensils, and even the use of the voice; in fact nothing is precluded. We read the following, by now a familiar statement:

> Musical awareness is much more likely to develop if, instead of having poor quality "educational music" drilled into him, the child is encouraged to make music of his own: guided by his teacher in musical principles by aural and notational training. (p. 3)

This is perhaps the most important statement from both musical and educational viewpoints. Musical things must do with musical awareness, and things educational with how to develop it. Somehow it seems to carry more weight coming from a German, the home of Beethoven and Bach, than from an American, the home of indeterminacy and John Cage as well as John Dewey and child centredness.

In the section on psychological research and its implications for the curriculum, the child's perceptions of the phenomena of sound, space, and time are mentioned. Compelling arguments are adumbrated in favour of a psychologically, rather than simply artistically, based approach to music through development of auditory perception. The whole notion is hinted at in very broad terms, inviting the reader to explore further. There follow some "practical applications in teaching" (p. 9). Here instruments and actions are listed and described. The use of various types of graphic symbols is advocated. Systematic approaches to identifying experiences are also an important part of the process. Part III comprises a number of experimental projects using a variety of traditional and modern notations, schemes, and improvisational activities, including graphic scores using colour.

This is a hard-hitting book in its fierce attack on traditional practises in music education, citing psychological and musical "evidence" in support. There are no excuses, no relenting, and no quarter given. It simply states that this approach to music education is the most logical, educationally defensible, and artistically viable.

A further book by Brian Dennis entitled *Projects in Sound* (1975) must be mentioned. This comprises twelve projects using a number of different stimuli to action. Notable is the collaboration of an artist in drawing appropriate graphic shapes — Oliver Bevan. The projects are intricate, detailed, and great fun, and here no attempt is made to justify or explain. This book is simply a set of projects involving visual and auditory experiences in an artistic setting.

Final comment is somewhat superfluous in that the variety and extent of experimental music in the classroom as exemplified by the publications listed and described here are self-evident. What is necessary now is to identify some educational and musical arguments that can help to clarify for the teacher what should constitute musical education in the classroom. Clearly it must be more than simply a set of recipes, and there must be compelling educational and musical arguments for any selection of material whether traditional or contemporary.

8

ISSUES OF TRADITION AND INNOVATION

Concepts of Quality

EARLIER chapters have exposed some issues surrounding musical quality, the impact of religion, the effects of new techniques in technology and science, and the growth of new practises in music. The purpose was to explain how at different times in history there have been musical practises with sufficient contrast in use of musical materials as to preclude the possibility of identifying universal values. Each historical time tends to generate its own set of values influenced by many factors both musical and nonmusical. In particular the influences of social and political events have always been in evidence in artistic practises. Throughout the history of Western thought and practise there have been numerous controversies concerned with the introduction of new practises in the arts, and many have been centred around religious or other social issues. Even today, it is argued, the supporters of the old and denigrators of the new often tend to defend their positions for reasons that have more to do with aesthetic values founded upon religious uses of music in earlier times and the deeply felt associations of meaning that have resulted than with any intrinsic merit of musical statement.

To recapitulate some of the points from earlier chapters, it was argued that aesthetic values emanating from the eighteenth century had two origins. These were love of elegance and simplicity fostered by the aristocratic ruling classes, and the use made of the resultant music by the church eager to evangelise. In the former the aristocratic classes attempted to re-create Hellenic concepts in their lifestyles, while in the latter the church's reformists found that musical participation of the people was now possible with the new "simple" musical style. The old art music of the Renaissance was too complex, but the rise of new tonal melodies and simple harmonies provided music well suited for massed singing. Many of Mozart's melodies were made into hymns and sung all over the world, so it was not just that the new style facilitated the growth of hymn singing but that such practises using the work of composers such as Mozart tended to establish a connection between religious usage and the work of masters. Such a connection gave powerful credence to certain types of music at the expense of others. In this instance it was tonal music centred on the major/minor scale system that began to gain powerful support as the true replacement of the modal system, which had held sway for many centuries. Thus the conceptual basis for musical structure was replaced during the seventeenth and eighteenth centuries by new concepts.

There was controversy surrounding the early growth of tonal music in the seventeenth and eighteenth centuries just as there was with de Vitry's "Ars Nova," referred to in earlier chapters. The latter shook the established views of the church in the fourteenth century, particularly over its attitudes towards the "profane" rhythm of two beats per measure as opposed to the theologically justified three beats, which related to teachings about the Trinity. The arguments were of course theological but clothed in musical symbolism. Today's controversies are not overtly concerned with theological issues in the sense that de Vitry's opponents' were, but the link suggested between religious usage, and therefore associated meaning, and eighteenth century concepts of elegance and simplicity is still powerful.

Some contemporary composers incorporate new sounds, or sounds not normally associated with historical musical practises, into their compositions. Their critics attack them on grounds of quality, judgement, and aesthetic taste. Consequently the noises of John Cage taken from everyday life, or the electronic sounds of

Stockhausen taken from the latest technology are not seen by some simply as responses to the contemporary by the contemporary but as instrusions into a musical world where values have already been established through the sanctification processes referred to and cannot be altered. In this way Cage or Stockhausen is no different from de Vitry in his challenge to prevailing orthodoxy.

What does this mean for music education? It cannot mean that the past should be buried in favour of everything new and contemporary. It does suggest that at the very least there is likely to be music of value in the contemporary scene. Since it is argued that the values relating to historical music might be invalid except in the religious or social context referred to it is necessary to suggest what might be valid if the religion-inspired aesthetic is considered unsuitable. It is certainly not easy to imagine how this can adequately address the concepts surrounding much of contemporary art music. One has either to reject the religion-inspired aesthetic or the contemporary art if the former is used as a criterion for judgements of the latter. The arguments put forward in earlier chapters suggest that different criteria have to be applied to different types of music. There is no evidence of universal criteria. Musical meaning is a product of enculturation, and as Westrup (1967) says, music "seems to be one of the most important ways man's nature expresses itself." Since man's nature is to expand his horizons and seek out new worlds both spiritual and physical, the implications for education are that music must be seen as an activity reflecting particular cultures, including the work of an individual artist as a kind of subdivision, the group he may exist in as another, and all subsumed within a larger cultural unit. These are the forces that shape musical practises and determine their meaning. When a Cage or de Vitry comes along it must be expected that prevailing ideas are not just going to be challenged but possibly changed eventually. The resultant controversy then becomes a battle to preserve the familiar against the attacks of the new. Thus the "Ars Nova" of the fourteenth century rose to preeminence, yet it too became a victim of change as the later practises of the Renaissance took over. The history of Western music is a history of ideas each supplanting a previous one to some degree or other. It certainly is not a history of stable values and unchanging ideas of excellence. As ideas as to what constitutes art change so examples of excellence will reflect this. For example, if one accepts Debussy's view of sonata form as potentially boring and repetitious it means that there can be some dull examples of sonata form, and use of it does not guarantee excellence. It also means that excellence can exist in other forms, or even that music that is possibly chaotic in one type of formal sense can have excellence if other criteria are available. Indeed the demise of eighteenth century tonality resulted in the demise of its tonal structures, notably sonata form. One cannot, therefore, criticize a symphony for its lack of tonal logic if the composer has used nontonal elements. Other criteria have to apply.

It can thus be argued that both on a micro and a macro level music should be viewed as an artistic activity without universal values applicable across all levels and styles. Thus on a micro level Stravinsky cannot be judged from criteria applicable to Beethoven, or Stockhausen from those to Mozart, or the music of the "Ars Nova" from those to late twentieth century. On a macro level it is equally impossible to apply judgements to aboriginal music from those applicable to music from Western culture. Westrup's comment that a discussion of music cannot possibly be regarded as irrelevant to the history of mankind (Chapter 2) takes on a new significance. As far as educational practises are concerned this is considerable. It means that we need to present music in education in the context of the history and praxis of man's various life-styles in many different cultures, or as something relevant to the culture the student lives in, exists in, thinks from, and derives his cultural standards from.

Quality, it is argued, can occur in many guises, and it is not so much which guise but whether or not quality is present. In music education the most important thing is not to introduce students to one particular type of music but rather to ideas of artistic excellence, whatever the type. Thus jazz, pop, electronic, symphonic, polyphonic, etc., are all useful if the concept of quality is addressed adequately. Much of the tonal music in education in the guise of simplified versions of folk or traditional songs is of poor quality. It lacks style and proper historical context. Nevertheless it is often used because of mistaken assumptions that anything tonal is good.

Educational Practises

In terms of educational practises this has certain consequences. The desire for universal literacy, that is the ability to relate pitches or

rhythms to their standard notational forms, can be seen in a historical context as part of a strategy whereby the church could more effectively disseminate religious doctrine through songs. It certainly
had its origins in this, as Chapters 3 and 4 have explicated. So what
can be the underlying reason for continuing this practise as the basis
of a general musical education for all children? It has been argued
that one reason can be found in the historical origins of modern education where music played such an important role, and the contention is that music in schools has been less affected by the ideas that
have shaped and altered educational perspectives of other activities.
It is, therefore, necessary to ask why we should continue to spend so
much time teaching a literacy that relates to historical musical practises.

Applying the conclusions relating to the central importance of
culture in shaping music there can only be justification for such
teaching if the aim is to teach historical music, or music that is historical in idiom. The question then arising is why should we teach
historical music! There can surely be little doubt that it is essential
we teach about our history in order that we know how we have arrived at this point, so perhaps the only question concerns at what
stage in the education process we ought to teach about historical music. This is not the only issue, however. There is a parallel one: What
should be the role of contemporary music in a general education?

Arguments were put forward in Chapter 7 for the use of contemporary idioms in the general music classroom, based upon both musical and educational criteria. Some of the ideas reflected an
ambivalence in that it was felt necessary to have a mixture of both
historical and contemporary music. This is certainly more healthy
than a fixed predilection for either to the exclusion of the other. The
issue though is educational effectiveness and relevance. Here common sense and experience teaching children would suggest that children have difficulty relating to a Mozart symphony without some
background, both sociocultural and musical. Similarly it can be observed that children easily relate to the latest popular recording often
without being too critical or aware of its musical content in any objective sense. Underlying such comments is a belief that one aim of
education is to enable people to stand back from objects and view
them critically so as to understand their own responses. Such objec-
tivity is not possible without some knowledge of the past, of the

forces that tend to shape our perceptions, and of contemporary issues that challenge them. It now becomes a matter of what we imagine a good education to be. This takes us outside the realm of music to a much broader scene.

Renaissance views of an ideal education certainly included music among the valued areas of study. Here there was little concerning aesthetic notions, merely a strong emphasis upon the social advantages of musical performance. To this end an ability to read music so as to be able to participate in a performance of a part-song was regarded in the sixteenth and seventeenth centuries as essential in the education of a gentleman (Morley, 1597). The aims were thus not so much musical as social. Music was seen as an element in socialization, not a discipline in its own right. The idea was that good social interactions could be helped and fostered through group participation in musical performances. There is evidence that today this idea is still prevalent, yet as anyone who has ever participated in such a group can testify as soon as questions of standards and professionalism leading to performance arise, the socialization value can easily diminish in inverse proportion. Here I am referring to modern recreations of the sixteenth or seventeenth century milieu using music of that period. In those times the use of methods for developing musical literacy was seen as a vital necessity, but in this age where there is so much emphasis upon standards and professionalism, and where live and recorded music are now an integral part of musical life, there are not the same social imperatives. Should such a renaissance milieu be fostered in schools? If so what would be the musical value? Can we say that such an activity has musical, social, or historical value?

John Locke (*see* Chapter 3) pointed out the weakness of such an ideal when he spoke of the time it takes to gain even a "moderate skill" in music. We do not live in an age where there is this amount of time for "nonproductive" activities. The rise of industrial society has fostered life-styles that gives us little time for activities that do not relate to wealth producing. Consequently there is a need for the professional musician whose function it is to amuse, entertain, or move our feelings. Thus there is a tendency to compartmentalise, and it does mean that there is not the opportunity for a development of individual skill in performance except for those who are going to make it their living or are prepared to devote a great deal of time and energy. It is certainly not an activity for the general classroom.

We can also see in this modern situation traces of educational structures that emerged in the eighteenth century and became the norm in the nineteenth. This was where the mass of industrial producers were educated according to their perceived function in society, to do with keeping their work rate up, not complaining, and becoming good, upright citizens by gladly fulfilling their role as workers. Indeed, the work of scientists promoting the biological determinist view of humanity in the nineteenth century and that of the intelligence testers relating to heredity in this century have reinforced such educational ideas (*see* Gould, 1981). Accordingly their music education was concerned with notions of soothing the savage beast, socialization, and religious indoctrination as illustrated in Chapter 3. By contrast those who were the organizers of society, the owners of industrial concerns or those who profited from them, had a musical education that had different aims. There was still the element of indoctrination and socialization but of a different type, and there was another that encouraged performance, composition, and the learning of skills relevant to the current state of the art of music. We have inherited this dichotomy and have not yet come to terms with its consequences in our educational practises.

Society is now in a different social situation. Today there is not such a clear-cut differentiation of such roles within society. Moreover there is now a greater ethnic mix found in any large city or community anywhere in the world. This causes further complications than those relating to the distinction between the past and the present within a particular culture. For an indigenous North American Indian it is not simply a matter of coping with European historical music in his education, for in addition he faces an alien (to him) notion of what music's function should be, notwithstanding that he would use sound in very different ways to a European.

Some of the most powerful arguments in modern education are those supporting the concept of a liberal education where the arts have an important function. Central to this is the need to educate the mind. Thus education becomes something that has an effect on the way we think, the way we view the world, the way we make judgements about the world. In particular the intellectual debate around moral judgements has served as a paradigm for deciding what the notion means for all subjects in the curriculum. The acquisition of a skill becomes a process serving the greater one to do with mind. The institutions that traditionally have produced the world's leaders have tended towards this approach.

Another powerful school of thought relates to the empirical view of human behavior found in the work of the so-called behavioural psychologists. Their influence can be seen in the notions of curriculum planning, sequencing, and predicting behaviours in the educative process. Yet another perspective shows a conflict between the progressivists and the traditionalists. The former advocate child centredness in shaping the curriculum, whereas the latters' concern is with preserving subject content rather than that which the child thinks he might want to learn.

It is not difficult to find one or more practises in music education that can be fitted to all the various ideas about the nature of education. Some have already been suggested. The MMCP relates quite readily to North American concepts of child-centred education, while the Kodaly choral method can be seen to fit well with the behavioural psychologists' concern with instructional strategies. The real interest for this writer concerns the nature of music as a means of communication rather than any particular educational theory. In fact it is argued that no single educational theory can adequately address the issues of music education unless it is fully cognizant of the practises of musicians. The Kodaly method demonstrates that it is possible to devise instructional strategies dealing with a sequence of behaviours in learning, e.g. pitch or rhythm concepts, and that such a sequence will prove highly effective in developing appropriate behaviours. Yet one cannot be wholly satisfied with the product, since there appears no significant attempt in the method to deal with the development of the mind. At least the rather trivial melodies that children are asked to sing appear to lack adequate sophistication for this.

There is organizational or even political value in addressing the problem of education's content and purpose in a general sense. To this end any institution can develop a coherent philosophy. Problems arise, however, as one attempts to fit individual subject areas into such a philosophy. Often it means compromise of content in the interests of the general philosophy. The history of music education outlined earlier in this book illustrates something of the distortion that can occur when pedagogues seek to fit content to an overriding philosophy. The arguments in Chapter 7 show that even with the introduction of contemporary music this problem is not entirely overcome. Some argue for its use on the grounds of relevance to contemporary practises in music, while others support its use because of its suitability in creative activities thought to be conducive to a liberal education or a child-centred one.

It is the contention of this writer that the problems identified in this book concerning music education in the general classroom can only be addressed effectively by examining the nature of musical practises, the musician's use of acoustic materials, the nature of a musical communication involving the originator, the executant, and the receiver, and the forces that conspire to give music its meaning. To this extent it is argued that the more general educational problem can be most effectively addressed from an understanding of the specific nature of the art of music. In other words knowledge in music can only come about through experience of the logic of musical discourse. While it may be argued that the human organism uses basically the same perceptual strategies in dealing with all phenomena, it is also suggested that these strategies are adjusted and adapted to suit the peculiar logic systems of different phenomena. To this extent the human organism appears infinitely adaptable. The auditory phenomena of music do comprise special logic systems.

The Growth and Decay of Logic Systems Peculiar to Music

To illustrate further the compelling influence of the contemporary on musical practises it is necessary to go no further than a comparison of different structures drawn from within Western art music. During the fifteenth and sixteenth centuries the concept of structure in music was derived from the verbal text and the manner in which it was set to music. Simply this meant that the text was broken up into short phrases and each was assigned rhythmic and melodic shape. The sections of a composition were thus delineated in the working through of the verbal phrase by each vocal or instrumental part. As each part finished the musical treatment of the words so the section was brought to a close. At this point a new section was begun by new words and a new musical phrase. In instrumental music this was adopted as a structural device with composers working through melodic phrases as though words were there and sectionalising the composition in the same way. Such a structure tends to be fragmented and to have no inner linear logic to carry it over long periods, with the consequence that pieces of this type tend to be short.

By contrast the lengthy essays in tonal logic of the eighteenth and nineteenth centuries have a quite different logical structure. In symphonic forms the structural logic of tonality enables a composer to address a whole universe of relationships inherent in key relatedness and tonic-dominant functions. The rise of tonality enabled J.S. Bach to imbue the fugue, a structural procedure typical of the fragmented type described above, with an inner linear logic system. The intellectual attractiveness of this logic system has prompted many to write about a language of music based upon tonal practises and inferred meanings. Yet many composers rejected it by the end of the nineteenth century as musically bankrupt and sought to find alternatives to its by then tortuous and ever increasing complexity, or in some cases vacuous length and empty rhetoric. Symphonies had grown so large that they lasted for an hour or more. Key relationships had grown so complex that it became difficult for the listener to grasp the subtleties of some structures. Composers resorted to many devices to hold together the concept of tonal logic. Brahms tried the introduction of a seventeenth century compositional device, the passacaglia, in his fourth Symphony, while Beethoven had already introduced the fugue into his compositions.

By the beginning of the twentieth century composers were looking for alternatives to the by then extremely cumbersome structures of tonality. Partly as a reaction to the giant structures of the nineteenth century, composers such as Debussy looked to a kind of anti-structural logic; he merely presented a series of acoustic ideas, each following on from the other. Some, "Les Six" in France, for example, went to extremes by producing short structures — five-minute operas. Webern in his *Bagatelles for String Quartet* produced structures of such brevity that their length can only be counted in seconds. It was not a return to the sectionalised structures of the Renaissance but an entirely new kind of structural logic, which in turn has motivated more recent composers such as Karlheinz Stockhausen and Pierre Boulez. This is explained more fully in Chapter 6.

The situation thus described is not due to any historical logical progression of ideas but rather to changing perceptions and fashions in the art of Western music. Some nonmusical influences at work have been identified in Chapter 6, and it can thus be deduced that composers work to principles that can only be defined and understood in terms of musical practises and how these are seen as a response to the conditions under which composers live. In other words it is argued that although musicians will always produce music, *de facto,* they will tend to shape the music to the situation they are in rather than to some higher order of values derived from some remote universal law of music. This of course makes it irksome for educational planners to devise curricula. It is difficult to establish definitive criteria from contemporary practises because, as has already been pointed out, these tend to be very diffuse and are continually being added to. It is, however, relatively easy to establish such from historical music because its complete corpus cannot be added to; it is fixed and immutable. The educationist needs to respond sensitively to this. Nevertheless a general education in music that is derived from musical practises must be concerned with the different logic structures referred to, and the acquisition of mere basic literacy skills is a poor substitute.

Cognition of Music

In earlier chapters there was reference to the cognitive musician, someone who relies upon cognition of musical sounds rather than active participation in producing them. In this role one can be a performer or a nonperformer. The cognitive musician perceives two categories of information: one can be described as concerned with the sensation of sound and the other with deeper structural content. The former has to do with a ravishing melody of Rachmaninov, the high drama of a Mahler symphony, the haunting strains of a tenor saxophone, the thrill of a large pipe organ heard in a medieval cathedral, the fascinating strangeness of music from other cultures, the electrifying beat of rock, the pulverising effect of a jazz drummer, etc. The latter is concerned with structural logic over the whole length of a piece of music, whether a fugue of Palestrina or Bach, a symphony of Mozart or Haydn, or a moment form of Stockhausen, etc. It can be argued that the first type is relatively uneducated in the sense that it is not necessary to have had a formal education to be able to perceive and appreciate such things. The second type, however, requires a formal education to be able to develop such sophisticated intellectual abilities. From this it can be stated that here are two basic levels of musical cognition: one to do with sensation, the other with structure. Common sense would indicate that sensation is more accessible to people than structure, and in any education process its use should precede studies in structure. The implication is clear: In music education in the general classroom the sensation of sound must be the focus that precedes education in music's structural logic systems. At the simple level of a young child's music education in the early grades, this means that the child should be given experiences in the nature of the phenomenon of sound before he is introduced to a developed language system of music.

Supporting evidence for such a conclusion can be drawn upon from within the practises of music and what we know of acoustic effects upon listeners. The history of music shows, for example, that composers have been drawn to new sounds as much by an interest in their acoustic properties as by their potential for incorporating some new structural logic. Mozart's fascination for the sound of the clarinet, a new instrument of his time, was based upon its acoustic properties and a desire to use them, presumably so that others could share the pleasure. It would certainly be controversial to imply that the clarinet had any impact on the development of the concerto except that Mozart wrote one of the first concertos for it. He liked the clarinet sound, so he wrote music for it, and the concerto idea was contemporaneous.

The development of piano music by composers at the beginning of the nineteenth century, when the instrument had overcome technical problems through the introduction of devices such as the check action and the iron frame, was characterized by explorations of its enormous expressive range as compared with that of the harpsichord. In earlier times the sonorous qualities inherent in the marvelous acoustics of St. Mark's Cathedral in Venice inspired Renaissance composers such as the Gabrielis and Monteverdi to exploit the situation by writing what is often called spatial music. The deployment of various groups of brass instruments or voices in galleries around the building gave rise to a new phenomenon of acoustic experience with simple chord patterns played or sung and coming at the listener from all sides. The development of this sensual experience into new musical logical structures came later through concertante — the deployment of constrasting instrumental sounds within an orchestra. Similarly the sonorities of the piano inspired relatively loosely structured pieces such as impromptus, bagatelles, and musical moments merely as vehicles for the ravishing sound of the piano. The point is argued, therefore, that in the practises of music, certainly in Western culture, there is evidence that even with the sophisticated mind of musician trained in music's structural logic an interest in the acoustic experience precedes that of a concern with deeper structural significance. A new sound will fascinate first, then become material for logical discourse in music.

Looking at what we know of primitive music there is clear evidence of a mystique surrounding the sounds heard by primitive man. Certain sounds were believed to be possessed of certain powers, and it is the acoustic property of the sound that is the focus, not just an arbitrary allocation of meaning, for some instruments were preferred above others by virtue of their acoustic quality.

It can be argued that an epistomological progression can be identified in music. This would be from the sensation of sound through to the most sophisticated structural logic where reliance upon acquired cognitive strategies is greater than upon untutored auditory sensory input.

9

A GENERAL MUSIC EDUCATION
A Synthesis and Final Comment

· PEDAGOGY AND THE ART OF MUSIC

GEORGE Bernard Shaw once commented that only "a fool's brain digests art into pedantry." He was not necessarily implying that the music educators who have produced methods for the development of musical skills from Guido onwards were all fools, but rather that it is foolish to imagine one can learn much about an art purely from pedagogy. The only way to learn about art is to experience and practise it. Institutions do not in themselves produce artists, but they can aid the development of such creative, sensitive beings by providing an atmosphere conducive to the unique development of such individuals.

In institutions of any kind there are pressures other than those concerned with professional practises, whether artistic or otherwise. Too often there tends to be an uneasy compromise between the needs of the individual student and the demands of management and organization. The previous chapters have shown how institutionalised pedantry has grown over the centuries in music education, often

motivated more by social and political than by artistic consider-
ations. In the general classroom today there is a clear lack of direction and purpose in music teaching, and the reasons are complex.
Pedantry has become so entrenched that art does not flourish in the
classroom. Schools generally seem to have difficulty with musical art
if it is not seen as serving church or state.

In recent times the emergence of art for art's sake has usurped an
older tradition of art serving a social or political institution. An artist
writing or painting for himself is a thoroughly modern situation.
This has undoubtedly produced conflict between a populace aesthetically still in the age of patronage, where an artist is expected to
please or entertain and an artist who produces art for his own aesthetic goals, irrespective of whether he pleases, challenges, or dis-
turbs. In education this conflict is reflected in the confusion
resulting from the widespread use of methods that relate to a past
age when music served a political or social purpose, and the existence in today's society of artists who serve different masters — themselves.

It is not that during the past musicians failed to address anyone
but their patrons, whether the church or the aristocratic ruling
classes, but rather that today an artist can be overtly addressing anyone who cares to listen; he does not have to look for the reaction of a
patron to the content of his music. He can establish himself as an
original, independent artist. This is not to say that there is no pressure to conform exerted on the artist today, merely that the emphasis
has shifted in the directions indicated. The significance of this for
music education is that the purpose for its existence in schools should
also have shifted ground but has not. Schools generally cling to ideas
concerning music education that were valid at some time in the past,
but no longer are, as support for activities that relate more to the historical than the contemporary. In the context of a general education
this is somewhat mistaken if we accept that one purpose of education
is to facilitate understanding of the world in which we live.

Musical Literacy

Most music education in the general classroom relates to developing concepts of literacy, but a literacy that relates to a historical
function of both music and education. In such a context literacy

means no more than being able to respond in the form of simple acts in pitch and rhythm production to musical notation developed in response to historical musical practises. The term *literacy*, however, implies far more than superficial acts in the form of mechanically realising in sound some simple configurations of pitch or rhythm notations, whether or not the idiom is historical. Literacy implies some understanding of the deep meanings associated with musical statements, some awareness of the composer's use of musical symbolism in the context of a style and semantic content associated with an individual composer. To use an analogy with language, if all that literacy meant was the development of an ability to make word sounds to printed letters on a page then a literate society would mean a society of people who could read road signs and other simple instructions with understanding but to whom the deep language structure and associated meanings of a story by John Steinbeck would be incomprehensible. In music this would mean a society of people who could sing a simple melody at sight with accuracy but who could not comprehend the structures and musical meanings of Beethoven's symphonic thought, Bach's contrapuntal, Stockhausen's, Cage's, John Coltrane's, "Yardbird" Parker's, etc. Yet these are the objects that literacy should be concerned with. Simple acts of interpreting basic symbols in rather trivial and contrived configurations of pitch and rhythm, devoid of expressive content or style, do not in themselves induce a state of literacy.

Composers and performers have something to communicate for those with "ears to hear." The main function of music educators in the general classroom is to facilitate the development of an ability to hear what musicians have to say. Music education in the general classroom, should, therefore, be concerned with musical structures, with musical manipulations of sound, with developing an understanding of the ways in which composers have organised and structured sound into meaningful statements. This should be the primary focus, not the acquisition of basic skills in making sounds in the interpretation of basic notations for pitch and rhythm. It is not to say that these can be dispensed with, but rather that the focus should be on matters of structure and semantic content and on the nature of sound as the means of communicating what Mendelssohn describes as "the thoughts . . . expressed by music . . . [which] . . . are not too indefinite to be put into words, but, on the contrary, too definite."

While it cannot be denied that an ability to read and understand orthodox notations can and does contribute something to the type of musical understanding referred to, it does not in itself enable this understanding to develop. Something more is required. Yet music education in the classroom seems to reflect a belief that it is only through an exhaustive training in the use of basic notational symbols that musical understanding can occur. Many of the music educators referred to earlier in this book have indicated that they seek to promote musical understanding in various guises, but significant is the body of opinion quoted in Chapter 7, which reflects a belief that studies of notation and associated behaviours contribute little to promoting understanding of the art of music. In particular this is true of those who support the use of contemporary musical practises in the classroom. Even those who tend to use historical idioms, e.g. Kodaly and Orff, betray a desire to do much more than merely develop simple behaviours without understanding. The argument is not, therefore, so much about the validity of developing musical understanding as how it can best be done.

Another perspective on some of the difficulties associated with attempting to develop understanding through existing literacy programs can be illustrated by comparing the musical content of such programs with the children's experiences of music outside school. A comment concerning the triviality of much that children are asked to perform in activities relating to basic literacy has already been made. The use of folk song, simplified melodically and rhythmically in children's school music books, is obviously an attempt to give some kind of meaning to acts of literacy. That such folk songs have to be simplified so that children can sing or play them tends to invalidate them as exemplars of musical practises. Simplifications of indigenous folk music are not a proper context for melody and rhythm, since they are neither genuine art nor folk music. Many of the complexities and subtleties of folk music are impossible to transcribe into orthodox Western notation, and injustice is done to the original by attempts to do this. Moreover, children's responses to music in the cinema tend to suggest they have greater intellectual capacity than is at present used in the classroom.

Children of any age seem to have little difficulty relating to complex concepts from the nineteenth century symphonic repertoire if presented in the context of a movie such as *E.T.*, or *Star Wars* yet might balk at the thought of listening to Tchaikowsky or Mahler in a performance of a complete symphony by either. The evidence from the cinema is that children readily take to hearing the most sophisticated music provided there is a context to which they can relate. They can listen to a Bach toccata or a Stravinsky ballet, as Walt Disney's *Fantasia* has demonstrated. Disney provided a way into the music through his use of visual matching of sound in the form of his cartoon figures. Such aids are clearly of some value to the musically unsophisticated mind, but so is the fact that children will listen and look while such sophisticated music is being performed of some value to the educator in assessing the aesthetic capabilities of children.

Another example will illustrate the significance of context in enabling children to respond to sophisticated musical statements. This was observed by the writer when he took his nine-year-old son, together with six other nine-year-old boys, to see the movie *Grease*. Near the beginning of the movie are a song and setting straight out of a romantic gothic novel where the heroine, having been treated roughly in public by the hero, sings of her devotion to him despite everything. The background is a garden with a romantic mood, and an overtly sentimental song is sung by the "pop" star Olivia Newton-John — "Hopelessly Devoted to You." Despite the "pop" cult surrounding her and John Travolta at that time, one might reasonably have expected mischievous nine-year-old boys to squirm at the exaggerated sentimentality. Instead there was a hush in the cinema and the nineteenth century romantic devices from the art of German lieder had their effect. The opening phrase of the song has a clear bass line with some predominatly minor harmonies moving towards the first phrase of the tune, which is based on the interval of the third. This is important, for the opening motif, making heavy use of chromatic auxiliary notes, employs thirds with much use of portamento. A sudden dramatic modulation to the flat submediant gives added poignancy to the "hopeless devotion" being expressed. Thus the structure and content of the song can be explained in terms that might apply to an analysis of a Schumann or Brahms lied. Certainly the thematic unity achieved in the use of the thirds both in the introduction and the melodic shape of the melody, together with the modulation to the flat submediant are not untypical of lieder. Doubtless had the song been presented as authentic lieder there would not have been the same response from the children. These nineteenth century idioms were given a twentieth century "flavour" by the additions of a rhythmic underlay and instrumentation, which a nineteenth century ear would not have experienced. There were some very twentieth century "pop" sounds from the singer, which no doubt helped the digestion of the nineteenth century idioms that surrounded them.

Even more interesting was the transmogrification of the heroine from the nineteenth century helpless female archetype, as characterized in the song just described, to the aggressive modern woman whose boyfriend had better "shape up," because she "needs a man" as she sings towards the ends of the story. The music is very modern, very twentieth century, and gone is the nineteenth century sentimentality. There was little doubt that the nine year olds had taken the point both of the heroine's character change and of the music's reflection of the essence of this change. Here was a use of musical symbolism in the context of this movie, which illustrated well the significance of semantic content in musical structures; nine year olds were able to perceive this!

Thus they were in fact being educated musically but without the formal instruction that enables them to understand matters of style, content, and musical semantics. Such experiences are not confined to children. It is quite possible that in this century generation after generation has had its emotional and aesthetic education from the media, principally the cinema, while the schools concentrate on what has become known as the "basics." To have an experience at all is something to be pleased about, for in past ages the masses had no real exposure to aesthetic experiences in the arts. Thus the millions who saw *Grease* had experience of the affective uses of melody, harmony, rhythm, accompaniment motifs, and instrumentation, not from the works of acknowledged great composers of German lieder but from extremely clever adaptations of this art form used in a context that had strong popular appeal. There was no educator on hand to help with organizing and analysing such an experience or responses in critical fashion, to explain what kind of musical art it represented. The audience was given an experience that it liked but could not explain. Thus music is left as an object that one either likes or dislikes, not as something understandable in terms of its own logic systems. In this way the totality of musical education consists in a training in schools in the "basics" and a haphazard amalgam of musical experiences in the media, which people are increasingly unable to explain or rationalise. It becomes impossible, therefore, to know whether in fact *Grease* is good musical art or bad; for the public can only say whether it liked it or not. This is indeed a great pity when one considers the potential of the human brain.

Aims of a General Music Education

To be educated in music means principally to understand musical structure, the manifestations of musical thought in the manipulations of sound by musicians, and the effects of various cultural forces on the way a composer develops his own musical symbols from the infinite variety available. It can mean much more, however. In just the same way that many people learn how to paint, so they could learn how to compose music. It need not be such a passive involvment as merely apprehending the works of others.

The traditional reliance upon musical skill development in behaviours relating to historical idioms ignores the problems associated with the need for adequate exposure. The activities require a period of time best expressed in years and a regularity best enumerated in hours daily. This presents serious problems for the majority of schools and students. In the routine of an ordinary school such exposure is not feasible, even if it were educationally desirable. Somehow the burdensome practises of this traditional musical education have to be circumvented if the primary goal of developing musical awareness and understanding is not to be submerged in an overwhelming focus upon traditional notation and associated behaviours. As indicated in Chapter 7, such practises can be bypassed through the use of sound-producing agencies, materials or instruments that do not require either a complicated technique for producing sound or rigorous training in orthodox notation. Thus a violin or a clarinet may not be suitable but a xylophone, a drum, or the voice might.

In a classroom situation this means that every child should have some kind of instrument that is capable of producing sound. It may be that some children can play orthodox instruments; if so this is a bonus for which the teacher should be grateful. The important thing is that every child should have something to make a sound with in order that he can make a contribution to a musical structure, a musical statement, a musical manipulation of sound, etc. No child should be exluded from music on the grounds that he or she does not have specialist lessons on an instrument. The classroom should be a place where children make their own live music, learn about musical structure and musical thought, develop their own ideas in musical fashion, understand the true function of notation in relation to musical acts by employing it for their own purposes in notating the sounds and structures they produce, and above all be involved in musical actions and thoughts. Many of the ideas explicated in Chapter 7 indicate some of the possibilities available to teachers. It would mean, of course, that teachers would also have to act and think like musicians rather than mere pedagogues. The same educational process should be available to them in their professional education. Teachers should be encouraged to develop their own musicality, not in imitation of the archetypal nineteenth century fanatic for virtuoso technique by locking themselves away in a practise room with some instrument, but rather in a quest for understanding the structural logic systems of music, the ways in which musical logic interacts with the perceiver, the amazingly diverse effects of man's different cultures, and above all in acts of personal musical expressions.

The trained specialist musician teaching in the context of a general music lesson needs to learn how to refocus his vocational orientation towards similar ends. Indeed, one of the main contributory factors to the malaise in music education is the almost total exclusion of a type of music education at the tertiary levels that is not strictly vocational in the narrow sense of being aimed solely at the intending practitioner. The problems that the products of this type of education encounter as they drift to the schools in search of work center around the realisation that either their own musical education was hopelessly inadequate for use in schools or schools are institutions they are best out of. It need not be such a dismal scenario. The prospect of reorientation should excite rather than daunt, for the responses of children are very rewarding when they are encouraged to compose and perform their own music.

Matters of educational structure and sequence, so much to the fore in the minds of the teacher, are very much at the mercy of the expertise and sensitivity artistically of the individual teacher. Art cannot be turned into pedantry without it ceasing to be art. A weakness of any scheme is a pretence to compensate for inadequencies of teachers in these matters by presenting structures that seek to take away the responsibility from the teacher for thinking, for planning, and for using his or her own sensitive awareness and experience in professional duties. This is what Shaw meant. No pedantry can adequately compesate for lack of artistic sensibility. Equally, no methodology, teaching structure, or sequence can succeed unless the teacher is clear about what he is doing, why he is doing it, and what he expects the children to gain from it. Music education in the general classroom should be a manifestation of the art of music, not a workshop in pedantry.

REFERENCES

American Orff-Schulwerk Association, Guidelines, 1980.

Arts Council of Great Britain: *Berlioz and the Romantic Imagination — A Guide to the Berlioz Exhibition,* 1969.

Biasini, Americole and Pogonowski, L.: *MMCP Interaction.* Bellingham, Americole, 1979.

Bruner, Jerome: *Beyond the Information Given.* New York, Norton, 1973.

Bryant, Peter: *Perception and Understanding in Young Children.* London, Methuen, 1974.

Cage, John: *Silence.* London, Calder and Boyars, 1968.

Choksy, Lois: *The Kodaly Method.* New Jersey, Prentice-Hall, 1974.

Congreve, William: (1697) from The mourning bride. Shapiro, Nat (Ed.): *An Encyclopedia of Quotations about Music.* New York, Da Capo Press, 1978.

Cooke, Deryck: *The Language of Music.* London, Oxford University Press, 1959.

Cott, Jonathan: *Stockhausen.* London, Robson, 1974.

Dalcroze, Emile-Jacques: *Rhythm, Music and Education.* London, Dalcroze Society, 1967.

Davies, John Booth: *Psychology of Music,* Stanford University Press, 1978.

Dennis, Brian: *Experimental Music in Schools.* London, Oxford University Press, 1970.

Dennis, Brian: *Projects.* London, Universal, 1975.

Evans, Peter: *The Music of Benjamin Britten.* London, Dent, 1979.

Gluck, Christof: Preface to *Alceste.* Quoted in Lawrence, Ian (1978).

Gould, Stephen J.: *The Mismeasure of Man.* New York, Norton, 1981.

Gregory, Richard: *Eye and Brain.* London, Wedenfeld, 1960.

Hall, Doreen: *Music for Children: Teacher's Manual.* London, Schott, 1960.

Halpern, Ida: Notes to *Ethnic Folkways,* library record album FE 4524, New York, 1974.

Hanslick, Eduard: *The Beautiful in Music.* Translated by G. Cohen New York, Bobbs-Merrill, 1957.

Harvey, Jonathan: *The Music of Stockhausen.* London, Faber, 1974.

Jeans, James: *Science and Music.* Cambridge, Cambridge University Press, 1961.

Julius, Ruth: Edgard Varèse. In Battcock, Gregory (Ed.): *Critical Anthology.* New York, Dutton, 1981.

Karkoschka, Erhard: *Notation in New Music.* London, Universal, 1972.

Keetman, Gunild: *Elementaria.* Murray, Margaret (trans.). London, Scholt, 1974.

Kodaly, Zoltan: *The Choral Method* (in several volumes). London, Boosey and Hawkes, 1965.

Kodaly, Zoltan: *The Selected Writings of Zoltan Kodaly.* London, Boosey and Hawkes, 1974.

Kostelanetz, Richard: *John Cage.* London, Allen Lane, 1978.

Kramer, Jonathan: Moment form. In Battcock, Gregory (Ed.): *Critical Anthology.* New York, Dutton, 1981.

Lang, Paul Henry: *Music in Western Civilization.* New York, Norton, 1941.

Lawrence, an: *Composers and the Nature of Music Education.* London, Scolar, 1978.

Ligetti, Gyorgy: Pierre Boulez. In *Die Reihe,* vol. 4, pp. 36-63. Bryn Mawr, Pennsylvania, Presser, 1960.

Malcolm, Norman and Von Wright, Georg H.: *Ludwig Wiltgenstein — A Memoir.* London, Oxford University Press, 1967.

Mendelssohn, Felix: Letter to Marc-Andre Sochay, 1842. In Morgenstern, Sam (Ed.): composers on music. New York: Pantheon, 1956.

Meyer, Leonard: *Emotion and Meaning in Music.* Chicago, University of Chicago Press, 1956.

Meyer-Denkmann, Gertrud: *Experiments in Sound.* London, Universal, 1977.

Miller, George: *Psychology, the Science of Mental Life.* London, Hutchinson, 1964.

Morley, Thomas: *A Plain and Easy Introduction to Practical Music.* Harman, R. Alec (Ed.). New York, Norton, 1953.

Orff, Carl: *Musik für Kinder* (5 volumes). Mainz, Schott, 1950-1954,

Orff, Carl: *Das Schulwerk.* Rückblick and ausblick. In Jahrbuch das Orff-Institut. Mainz, 1963.

Paynter, John and Aston, Peter: *Sound and Silence.* Cambridge, Cambridge University press, 1970.

Persichetti, Vincent: *Twentieth Century Harmony.* London, Faber and Faber, 1961.

Pratt, Carroll C.: *The Meaning of Music.* New York, Johnson, 1968.

Prelleur, Peter: *Modern Music Master.* Basel, Barenreiter, 1965. (Facsimile of 1731)

Radocy, Rudolf and Boyle, David: *The Psychological Foundations of Musical Behavior.* Springfield, Thomas, 1979.

Raebeck, Lois and Wheeler, Lawrence: *New Approaches to Music in the Elementary School.* Dubuque, Brown, 1980a.

Raebeck, Lois and Wheeler, Lawrence: *Orff and Kodaly.* Dubuque, Brown, 1980b.

Rainbow, Bernarr: *The Land without Music.* London, Novello, 1967.

Read, Herbert: *The True Voice of Feeling.* London, Faber, 1968.

Sandvoss, Joachim: *Orff's Music for Children.* Vancouver, Simon Fraser University, 1976.

Schafer, R. Murray: *The Composer in the Classroom*. Toronto, B.M.I., 1965.

Schafer, R. Murray: *Ear Cleaning*. Toronto, B.M.I., 1967.

Seimens, Margaret: Comparison of Orff and traditional methods in music. *J.R.M.E., 17,* 1969.

Self, George: *New Sounds in Class*. London, Universal, 1967.

Sergeant, Desmond: Measurement of pitch discrimination. *J.R.M.E., 21,* 1973.

Smalley, Roger: Stockhausen's moment form. *Musical Times,* 25-26, January, 1974.

Stockhausen, Karlheinz: *Texte,* bands 1 & 2. Vienna, Schauberg, 1963/4.

Thomas, Ronald: *MMCP Synthesis*. Bellingham, Americole, 1979.

Vajda, Cecilia: *The Kodaly Way to Music*. London, Boosey and Hawkes, 1974.

Walker, Robert: *Sound Projects*. London, Oxford University Press, 1976.

Walker, Robert: Unpublished survey of English cathedral choirs, 1974.

Wellesz, Egon: *Ancient and Oriental Music,* New Oxford History of Music, vol. 1. London, Oxford University Press, 1969.

Westrup, Jack: *Introduction to Musical History*. London, Hutchinson, 1967.

White, Eric: *Stravinsky*. London, Faber, 1966.

Whittall, Arnold: *Music Since the First World War*. London, Dent, 1977.

Winckel, Fritz: *Music, Sound and Sensation*. New York, Dover, 1967.

Witkin, Robert: *The Intelligence of Feeling*. London, Heinemann, 1974.

Wollheim, Richard: *Art and its Objects*. London, Penguin, 1968.

Wörner, K.H.: *Stockhausen*. London, Faber, 1973.

INDEX

A

Abstract symbols, 49, 50
Accents, 54
 acoustics, 53, 54, 43, 144
 aesthetics in music, 4, 7, 9, *12-22, 29-33*, 78, 127, 128, 132, 133, 134, 150
Africa, 69
African tribal music, 39
Alaska, 69
Alberti, D., 8
Aldeburgh Festival, 70
American music, 21, 71
American Orff-Schulwerk Association, 46, 48
 amplitude, 52, 53, 54, 55, 63, 64, 65, 67, 106
 amplitude modulation, 81
Antarctic, 69
 antique cymbals, 80
 antistructural logic in music, 141
 anvils, 78
 arpeggio, 51
"Ars Nova," 61, 63, 133, 134, 135
 art education, 111
 artist, 111
 art music, 50, 51, 59, 71, 75, 153
Asian musical cultures, 47
Aston, P., 110, 125, 127
 atomization of sound, 81, 89, 93
 auditory awareness, 107, 130, 144

 auditory sensation, 106, 144
Aus den seiben Tagen, 87
Australian Aboriginal music, 39
 autochthonous processes, 67
 avant-garde, 112

B

Bach, J.S., 5, 41, 96, 107, 116, 124, 130, 141, 142, 147, 149
Bagatelles, opus 9 (Webern), 89, 141
Bali, 40, 71, 73
 bamboo claves, 80
Bartok, Bela, 38, 75, 76, 81
 basic skills, 147
 basilar membrane, 55, 66
 bass drum, 76
 bass guitar, 83
Beethoven, L., vii, 15, 21, 41, 69, 70, 75, 77, 96, 100, 116, 125, 130, 135, 141, 147
Berio, L., 84, 110, 113
Berlin Philharmonic Orchestra, vii
Berlioz, h., 19, 75
Bernstein, L., vii
Bevan, Oliver, 131
Biasini, A., 113
 binary form, 90
 biological determinism, 138
"Birdland," vii, viii
 bongo, 80

Note: Italics indicate pages that carry in-depth discussions of the index entries.

159